Copyright © 2023 by Sophia M. Johnson (Author)
All rights reserved. No part of this book may be reproduced or utilized in any form or by any means, electronic or mechanical, including photocopying, recording or by any information storage and retrieval system, without permission in writing from the publisher, except for brief quotations in critical articles or reviews.

The content of this book is based on various sources and is intended for educational and entertainment purposes only. While the author has made every effort to ensure the accuracy, completeness, and reliability of the information provided, the information may be subject to errors, omissions, or inaccuracies. Therefore, the author makes no warranties, express or implied, regarding the content of this book.

Readers are advised to seek the guidance of a licensed professional before attempting any techniques or actions outlined in this book. The author is not responsible for any losses, damages, or injuries that may arise from the use of information contained within. The information provided in this book is not intended to be a substitute for professional advice, and readers should not rely solely on the information presented.

By reading this book, readers acknowledge that the author is not providing legal, financial, medical, or professional advice. Any reliance on the information contained in this book is solely at the reader's own risk.

Thank you for selecting this book as a valuable source of knowledge and inspiration. Our aim is to provide you with insights and information that will enrich your understanding and enhance your personal growth. We appreciate your decision to embark on this journey of discovery with us, and we hope that this book will exceed your expectations and leave a lasting impact on your life.

Title: Traditions to Transcend: Global Festivals for Renewal
Subtitle: Ceremonies, Rituals and Prayers

Series: Worldwide Wellwishes: Cultural Traditions, Inspirational Journeys and Self-Care Rituals for Fulfillment in the Coming Year
Author: Sophia M. Johnson

Table of Contents

Introduction 6
The Significance of New Year Festivals 6
Common Themes Across Cultures 9
Overview of Key Traditions 12

Chapter 1: Chinese New Year 16
Origins and Mythology 16
Preparations and Decorations 20
New Year's Eve Festivities 25
Customs for Luck and Prosperity 30

Chapter 2: Japanese New Year 36
Oshogatsu Traditions 36
Hatsumode Temple Visits 42
Lucky Foods 49
Joya No Kane: Bell Ringing for Reflection and Renewal ... 55

Chapter 3: Rosh Hashanah 64
Sweet Symbolism 64
High Holiday Rituals 72
Shofar Horn Blowing: A Call to the Soul 79
Tashlich Casting Off Sins: A Ritual of Renewal by the Water's Edge 89

Chapter 4: Diwali 96
Victory of Light Story: Illuminating the Spiritual Tapestry of Diwali 96

Clay Lamp Lighting: Illuminating the Sacred Path of Diwali 105
Feasts and Fireworks: A Banquet of Joy and Spectacle 113
Prayer Rituals: Illuminating the Spiritual Essence of Diwali 124

Chapter 5: Songkran 132
Water Festival Significance: Embracing Renewal and Joy in the Thai New Year 132
New Year Blessings: Invoking Prosperity, Harmony, and Good Fortune in Songkran 139
Parades and Parties: A Festive Tapestry of Joy in Songkran 146
Cleansing Rituals: Purification and Renewal in Songkran 153

Chapter 6: Nowruz 160
Zoroastrian History: Illuminating the Origins of Nowruz 160
Haft Seen Table Setting: A Symphony of Symbols in Nowruz 165
Out With the Old: Nowruz's Rituals of Purification and Renewal 171
In With the New: Nowruz's Resplendent Beginnings and Symbolic Traditions 177

Chapter 7: Hijri New Year 184

Islamic Calendar: Navigating Time with the Lunar Tapestry *184*
Crescent Moon Sighting: Illuminating the Islamic Calendar *189*
Reflection and Atonement: Embracing Spiritual Renewal *195*
Celebrations and Charity: Communal Joy and Compassionate Giving *202*

Conclusion **207**
Finding Unity in Diversity *207*
Carrying Traditions Into Future Generations *212*
Celebrating Our Shared Humanity *218*

Wordbook **224**
Supplementary Materials **227**

Introduction
The Significance of New Year Festivals

As we stand on the cusp of a new year, marked by the passage of time, humanity across the globe converges in a multitude of celebrations, each a vibrant tapestry woven with customs, rituals, and prayers. The significance of New Year festivals extends far beyond the ticking of the clock, delving deep into the heart of cultures, religions, and communities. In this exploration, we embark on a journey through time and tradition, unraveling the rich tapestry of festivities that unite us in our shared human experience.

Understanding the Essence:

New Year festivals serve as pivotal milestones in the collective human narrative, encapsulating the essence of renewal, hope, and the perpetual cycle of life. Beyond the temporal transition from one calendar year to another, these celebrations carry profound symbolic meanings deeply rooted in cultural and religious histories. They are a testament to our innate yearning for fresh beginnings, a chance to cast away the shadows of the past, and to embrace the promise of a brighter future.

Common Threads Across Cultures:

While diverse in their origins and practices, New Year festivals share common threads that weave through the fabric of humanity. Themes of light, fresh starts, and prayers for prosperity echo across cultures, forming a universal language that transcends geographical boundaries. Whether it's the mesmerizing spectacle of fireworks illuminating the night sky, the resonance of bells heralding new beginnings, or the sacred act of reflection and atonement, these festivals bind us in a shared celebration of the human spirit.

Overview of Key Traditions:

As we delve into the heart of this exploration, we will navigate through the intricacies of each celebration. From the exuberant festivities of Chinese New Year, steeped in ancient mythology and adorned with symbols of luck, to the serene contemplation of Rosh Hashanah, marked by the poignant sound of the shofar and the casting off of sins, each tradition offers a unique lens through which to view the world and our place in it.

In the chapters that follow, we will embark on a cultural odyssey, exploring the origins, mythology, preparations, and customs that define each New Year festival. From the bustling markets adorned with red lanterns in anticipation of the Chinese New Year to the serene temple visits during Oshogatsu in Japan, and the vibrant colors of Diwali illuminating the night in celebration of light's triumph over darkness — these traditions beckon us to uncover the stories etched in the annals of time.

Join us in this global journey of renewal, as we uncover the rich symbolism, partake in age-old rituals, savor the diverse flavors of festive feasts, and immerse ourselves in the collective prayers for prosperity. As we explore the customs that transcend borders, we find not only the beauty of our differences but also the profound unity that binds us all in the celebration of life, love, and the eternal hope embedded in the dawn of a new year.

Common Themes Across Cultures

In the kaleidoscope of global New Year festivals, a remarkable tapestry emerges, woven with threads of shared humanity that bind disparate cultures and religions together. As we navigate through the diverse celebrations spanning Chinese New Year to Rosh Hashanah, Diwali to Songkran, a profound realization unfolds—the resonance of common themes that transcend geographical borders and cultural nuances. This chapter unravels the intricate patterns of similarity that connect us all in the celebration of the new, the hope for prosperity, and the symbolic emergence from darkness into light.

Timeless Symbolism:

At the heart of these celebrations lies a universal symbolism, an acknowledgment of the cyclical nature of time and the perpetual journey of life. The turning of the calendar marks not only the passing of days but also an opportunity for rebirth and renewal. Whether it's the striking of a gong at midnight, the lighting of candles, or the symbolic act of casting off sins, these rituals echo the collective human yearning for a fresh start—a chance to leave behind the old and embrace the new.

Light as a Unifying Force:

One of the most captivating threads weaving through these celebrations is the symbolism of light. From the radiant lanterns of Chinese New Year to the glittering diyas of Diwali, the illumination of darkness stands as a powerful metaphor. It speaks to our shared desire to dispel shadows, both literal and metaphorical, and welcome the dawn of hope. Light, in its myriad forms, becomes a universal symbol of positivity, enlightenment, and the triumph of good over evil.

Prayers for Prosperity:

As the New Year unfolds, so too do the collective prayers for prosperity. Whether expressed through intricate rituals, solemn ceremonies, or joyous feasts, the desire for abundance and well-being unites cultures around the globe. From the heartfelt prayers for a bountiful harvest during Nowruz to the casting of wishes on the waters of Songkran, these acts of devotion reflect the shared human aspiration for a future filled with blessings, prosperity, and joy.

Reflecting on the Past:

Another common theme is the act of reflection and introspection. Across cultures, the advent of the New Year prompts a collective pause—a moment to contemplate the journey behind and envision the path ahead. Whether it's the Jewish tradition of Tashlich, casting off sins into flowing waters, or the Islamic practice of reflection and atonement during Hijri New Year, the acknowledgment of the past informs the aspirations for the future.

Joyful Celebrations:

Amidst the profound symbolism and reflection, New Year festivals are, at their core, celebrations of joy. Parades, parties, feasts, and communal gatherings become expressions of shared happiness, transcending linguistic and cultural barriers. The infectious energy of festivities, be it the lively water fights of Songkran or the exuberant drumming and lion dances of Chinese New Year, underscores the innate human inclination to come together in joyous revelry.

In the chapters that follow, we will delve into the unique expressions of these common themes, witnessing how cultures infuse their distinct flavors into the universal concepts of renewal, light, prosperity, reflection, and celebration. Join us on this cross-cultural exploration, where the diversity of traditions only deepens our understanding of the shared human experience—a global tapestry woven with threads of hope, joy, and the perennial quest for a brighter tomorrow.

Overview of Key Traditions

In the intricate mosaic of New Year celebrations worldwide, the beauty lies not just in the diversity of festivities but in the unique traditions that define each cultural tapestry. As we embark on this journey through time and tradition, let us pause to survey the breathtaking panorama of key customs that characterize the celebrations of Chinese New Year, Japanese New Year, Rosh Hashanah, Diwali, Songkran, Nowruz, and Hijri New Year. Each tradition, a brushstroke in the canvas of global celebrations, paints a vivid picture of cultural heritage, mythology, and the enduring spirit of renewal.

Chinese New Year: Embracing the Mythical Past

The Chinese New Year, a spectacle of red lanterns, dragon dances, and familial bonds, is steeped in a rich tapestry of mythology. As we unravel the origins of this celebration, we discover a world where mythical creatures and ancient deities mingle with the hopes and dreams of the present. From the meticulous preparations and vibrant decorations that blanket the streets to the solemn customs designed to invite luck and prosperity, Chinese New Year stands as a testament to the enduring connection between the past and the future.

Japanese New Year: Oshogatsu and the Serenity of Tradition

In Japan, Oshogatsu unfolds as a serene contemplation of the past year and a hopeful embrace of what lies ahead. Amidst the serene beauty of Hatsumode temple visits and the symbolic ringing of the Joya No Kane bells, the Japanese New Year exudes a sense of tranquility. Discover how lucky foods and age-old customs intertwine with a reverence for the divine, creating a celebration that seamlessly merges tradition with the contemporary spirit of renewal.

Rosh Hashanah: Sweet Beginnings and Spiritual Reflection

For the Jewish community, Rosh Hashanah marks not only the beginning of the new year but also a period of profound spiritual reflection. Delve into the symbolism behind the sweetness of apples and honey, the solemnity of shofar horn blowing, and the poignant Tashlich ceremony where sins are cast into flowing waters. Rosh Hashanah beckons us to witness the blend of joyous celebration and deep introspection that defines this High Holiday.

Diwali: Festival of Lights and Triumph Over Darkness

Diwali, the Festival of Lights, unfolds as a grand spectacle of victory over darkness and the triumph of good over evil. As we explore the Victory of Light story, witness the symbolic lighting of clay lamps, indulge in festive feasts, and marvel at the dazzling fireworks that illuminate the night sky. Diwali beckons us into a world where the radiance of a single diya symbolizes the eternal battle between light and darkness.

Songkran: Water, Blessings, and Joyous Celebrations

In Thailand, the Songkran Water Festival emerges as a vibrant celebration of water's cleansing power, blessings for the new year, and joyous communal gatherings. Explore the significance of water in cleansing rituals, join the exuberant parades and parties, and witness how Songkran transforms the ordinary act of water splashing into a profound symbol of renewal and purification.

Nowruz: Zoroastrian Roots and the Haft Seen Table Setting

Nowruz, heralding the arrival of spring, traces its roots to Zoroastrian traditions. Journey through the history of this festival, adorned with the symbolism of the Haft Seen table setting—a visual feast representing the seven elements of life. Experience the jubilation of "Out with the Old, In with the New" as communities come together to welcome the vernal equinox with open arms.

Hijri New Year: Lunar Cycles, Reflection, and Charity

The Hijri New Year follows the Islamic calendar, its celebration marked by the sighting of the crescent moon. Witness the reflective spirit of this occasion, where communities engage in introspection, seek forgiveness, and engage in acts of charity. Explore the unique aspects of the Islamic New Year celebration, where the lunar cycles become a guiding force in shaping the rhythm of life.

As we venture into the heart of each tradition, let us marvel at the diversity of expressions that encapsulate the universal themes of renewal, light, and prayers for prosperity. The upcoming chapters invite you to immerse yourself in the intricacies of these key traditions, discovering the profound beauty that lies in the details, the stories, and the enduring legacies that define the New Year celebrations across cultures.

Chapter 1: Chinese New Year
Origins and Mythology

In the vast tapestry of Chinese culture, the Chinese New Year stands as a radiant jewel, a celebration that echoes with the resonance of ancient myths and enduring traditions. As we step into the heart of this vibrant festival, it is imperative to journey back in time, unraveling the threads of mythology that weave through the origins of Chinese New Year. In the mythical landscape of ancient China, where dragons soared and celestial beings roamed, the foundations of this celebration were laid, giving birth to a cultural phenomenon that continues to captivate the world.

The Mythical Tapestry:

At the heart of Chinese New Year lies a tapestry woven with myths that traverse the realms of heaven and earth. One such myth centers around the ferocious Nian, a mythical beast said to emerge from the depths of the sea every New Year's Eve. Legend has it that Nian would devour crops, livestock, and even humans, leaving devastation in its wake. To thwart this menace, the ancient Chinese devised ingenious methods rooted in myth and superstition, setting the stage for the elaborate rituals that define the festival today.

The Monster and the Wise Elder:

As the Nian terrorized the villages, an elderly wise man emerged as a beacon of hope. Armed with knowledge passed down through generations, he discovered the creature's aversion to loud noises and the color red. Villagers, upon hearing this revelation, began using firecrackers, drums, and red decorations to fend off the Nian. The symbolic act of driving away the monster became an integral part of Chinese New Year, evolving into the spectacular displays of fireworks and the pervasive use of the color red in modern celebrations.

The Jade Emperor's Edict:

Beyond the earthly realm, Chinese mythology introduces us to the celestial court and the omnipotent Jade Emperor. As the legend goes, the emperor decided to establish a means of counting time, resulting in the creation of the Chinese zodiac. The twelve animals—Rat, Ox, Tiger, Rabbit, Dragon, Snake, Horse, Goat, Monkey, Rooster, Dog, and Pig—each represented a year in a twelve-year cycle. The order in which they completed a mythical race determined their place in the zodiac, shaping the destinies of those born under their influence.

The Great Race:

The Chinese zodiac's inception is intertwined with the tale of the Great Race, a competition organized by the Jade

Emperor. The animals, each vying for a coveted position in the zodiac, embarked on a race across treacherous terrain. The rat, known for its cunning nature, hitched a ride on the back of the diligent ox, securing its victory by leaping ahead at the last moment. Thus, the rat claimed the first year of the zodiac cycle, while the ox secured the second.

Symbolism in the Zodiac:

The Chinese zodiac is a repository of symbolic meaning, with each animal embodying distinct characteristics and traits. The dragon, a creature of myth and majesty, symbolizes power, luck, and success. In contrast, the rabbit exudes qualities of gentleness and compassion. These animal archetypes infuse Chinese New Year with a dynamic energy, influencing everything from personal characteristics to predictions for the year ahead.

Embracing Tradition in Modern Celebrations:

As the mythological origins of Chinese New Year unfold, they seamlessly merge with the vibrant tapestry of modern celebrations. From the dazzling parades featuring dragon and lion dances to the ubiquitous display of red lanterns and the explosive symphony of fireworks, the mythological roots persist in the pageantry of the festival. In contemporary China and among Chinese communities worldwide, the Nian is not just a mythical monster; it has become a symbol of overcoming challenges, a metaphor for confronting fears and ushering in prosperity.

In the chapters that follow, we will delve into the modern manifestations of these ancient myths, exploring how they shape the elaborate preparations, decorations, and customs that define Chinese New Year. The mythology that birthed this celebration continues to breathe life into the traditions, creating a cultural legacy that transcends time and connects generations in a shared celebration of renewal, hope, and the triumph of light over darkness.

Preparations and Decorations

As the lunar calendar ushers in the arrival of Chinese New Year, the air becomes electrified with anticipation, and communities come alive with a palpable energy. At the heart of this vibrancy lies a meticulous tapestry of preparations and decorations that transform homes, streets, and entire cities into a dazzling spectacle. The elaborate rituals and symbolic adornments are not mere gestures; they are a collective endeavor to invite prosperity, good fortune, and auspicious energies into the coming year.

Spring Cleaning and Renewal:

Preparations for Chinese New Year commence with a tradition deeply ingrained in the ethos of renewal—spring cleaning. Families embark on a thorough cleansing of their homes, sweeping away the remnants of the past year and making way for the fresh energy that the new year promises. Dust is swept away, windows are opened to allow stagnant energies to escape, and homes are adorned with vibrant decorations in anticipation of the festive season.

Red: The Color of Prosperity:

Central to Chinese New Year decorations is the resplendent color red. Symbolizing good luck, joy, and prosperity, red saturates the visual landscape of the festival. Red lanterns, banners, and intricate paper cutouts adorn homes and public spaces, creating a tapestry that radiates positive energy. The color red is not merely a visual spectacle; it is a powerful symbol believed to ward off evil spirits and invite blessings into the household.

Door Couplets and Auspicious Phrases:

Door couplets, known as "Chunlian," are a distinctive feature of Chinese New Year decorations. These are poetic phrases written on vertical strips of red paper and affixed to either side of the front door. The couplets convey good wishes, express hopes for prosperity, and invoke positive energies for the coming year. Crafting and displaying these poetic expressions is an art form in itself, with families carefully selecting or composing phrases that resonate with their aspirations.

Fu Character and Upside-Down Good Luck:

The character "Fu," meaning good fortune or happiness, is a ubiquitous presence in Chinese New Year decorations. Often displayed upside-down, the character takes on a dual meaning. When read phonetically, "upside-down" in Chinese sounds like "arrive," signifying the arrival of good fortune. The careful placement of the "Fu" character, often in the center of the front door or as part of decorations, is a deliberate act to invite auspicious energies into the household.

Paper Cutouts and Window Decorations:

The art of paper cutting, or "Jianzhi," finds prominence in Chinese New Year decorations. Delicate and intricate designs depicting animals, symbols, and characters are meticulously crafted and displayed on windows and walls. These paper cutouts not only add a touch of artistic elegance but are also believed to bring good luck and harmony to the household.

Traditional New Year Paintings:

Traditional New Year paintings, or "Nianhua," are artistic expressions that capture the spirit of the festival. These colorful artworks often feature auspicious symbols, deities, and scenes from Chinese mythology. Families display these paintings in their homes to invoke blessings, ward off negative energies, and infuse the living space with the positive vibes associated with the festival.

The Kitchen God and Offerings:

In the weeks leading up to Chinese New Year, households pay special attention to the Kitchen God, believed to oversee the family's kitchen and domestic harmony. As part of preparations, families offer sacrifices to the Kitchen God, symbolized by burning a portrait or effigy. This ritual is believed to send the Kitchen God to the heavens, reporting on the family's actions over the past year.

A positive report is said to bring good fortune in the coming year.

Traditional Attire and Auspicious Colors:

Personal preparations for Chinese New Year extend beyond the home to include the selection of traditional attire. Red, once again, takes center stage in clothing choices, symbolizing joy and good luck. Families often don new clothing, with elders gifting red envelopes, or "Hongbao," containing money, to younger members—a gesture believed to bestow blessings and prosperity.

Firecrackers and Drums:

As the eve of Chinese New Year approaches, the air is filled with the explosive sounds of firecrackers and the rhythmic beats of drums. This centuries-old tradition is rooted in the mythical origins of the festival, where the noise was believed to scare away the Nian monster. Today, firecrackers are an integral part of celebrations, signaling the banishment of negative forces and the joyous arrival of a new beginning.

Floral Decorations:

Floral arrangements play a significant role in Chinese New Year decorations, with certain flowers carrying specific meanings. Plum blossoms symbolize resilience and perseverance, while peonies represent wealth and prosperity.

Orchids embody refinement and beauty, and tangerine trees are believed to bring good luck and fortune. Homes and public spaces are adorned with these floral arrangements, creating an atmosphere that is both visually stunning and rich in symbolism.

In the chapters that follow, we will delve deeper into the significance of these preparations and decorations, exploring the stories, symbolism, and cultural nuances that make Chinese New Year a festival of profound depth and visual splendor. The careful orchestration of these elements is not merely a tradition; it is a collective expression of hope, a cultural symphony that resonates with the promise of prosperity and the embrace of the new year's blessings.

New Year's Eve Festivities

As the sun dips below the horizon on the eve of Chinese New Year, a transformative energy sweeps through China and Chinese communities worldwide. The anticipation crescendos, reaching its zenith as families gather, traditions are observed, and a sense of unity blankets the landscape. The New Year's Eve festivities mark a moment of profound significance—a threshold between the old and the new, a time for reflection, reunion, and the commencement of a joyous celebration that reverberates through the night.

Reunion Dinner: A Feast of Togetherness:

At the heart of Chinese New Year's Eve is the Reunion Dinner, or "Nian Ye Fan." Families come together from near and far to partake in this symbolic feast, emphasizing the importance of familial bonds and shared traditions. The meal is a lavish spread featuring an array of symbolic dishes, each carrying its own significance. Dumplings, representing wealth, and fish, symbolizing abundance, are staples on the New Year's Eve table. The feast is not merely a culinary delight; it is a ritual that binds generations and fosters a sense of unity.

Setting the Table: Symbolism and Tradition:

The act of setting the New Year's Eve dinner table is imbued with symbolism and tradition. Red tablecloths, symbolizing good luck, are often used, and the table is adorned with auspicious decorations. The central placement of a hot pot, known as "hotpot of reunion," encourages communal dining, fostering a spirit of togetherness. The meal itself is a carefully curated selection of dishes, each chosen for its symbolic significance and the positive energies it is believed to invoke.

Making Offerings to Ancestors:

Before the feast begins, families often pay homage to their ancestors by making offerings on the ancestral altar. The act of honoring the past is a poignant tradition, symbolizing gratitude for the wisdom and sacrifices of those who came before. Incense is lit, and offerings of food, tea, and other items are presented as a gesture of respect. This ritual not only connects the living with the departed but also acknowledges the continuity of family and cultural heritage.

The Midnight Moment: Welcoming the New Year:

As the clock approaches midnight, the atmosphere becomes charged with anticipation. Families gather around the television to watch the annual CCTV New Year's Gala, a televised variety show that has become an integral part of the Chinese New Year experience. The moment the clock strikes twelve is heralded by the explosive symphony of fireworks, marking the official arrival of the new year. The night sky is ablaze with color, and the streets reverberate with the resounding crackle of firecrackers—a collective spectacle that transcends regional boundaries and unites the nation in celebration.

Lucky Red Envelopes: A Gesture of Prosperity:

Following the stroke of midnight, elders in the family distribute red envelopes, or "Hongbao," to the younger members. These envelopes, often adorned with symbols of wealth and prosperity, contain money and are a symbolic gesture believed to bring good luck and blessings. The act of giving and receiving Hongbao is a cherished tradition, symbolizing the passing on of prosperity from one generation to the next.

Temple Visits and Religious Observances:

In the early hours of the new year, some families embark on visits to temples to seek blessings for the coming year. This tradition, known as "Bai Nian," involves paying respects to deities, making offerings, and participating in religious ceremonies. The temple visits are a blend of spirituality and cultural practice, providing a moment of reflection and gratitude for the blessings received.

Staying Awake to Usher in Good Fortune:

A unique tradition on Chinese New Year's Eve involves staying awake throughout the night, known as

"Shou Sui." This practice is believed to ward off evil spirits and ensure a long and prosperous life. Families engage in various activities to stay awake, such as playing games, watching fireworks, and sharing stories. The act of staying awake is not only a cultural tradition but also a joyful celebration that bridges the old and the new.

First Footing: Welcoming Good Fortune:

In some regions, the concept of "First Footing" is observed, where the first person to enter a home after midnight is believed to bring good fortune for the coming year. This individual, known as the "First Footer," is often chosen for their positive energy and auspicious characteristics. The act of First Footing is a lively and joyous custom, symbolizing the invitation of prosperity and happiness into the household.

The Red Lanterns and Nian Monster Folklore:

As the night unfolds, the streets come alive with the warm glow of red lanterns, casting a magical ambiance over the surroundings. According to folklore, the Nian monster, fearing the color red, is banished by the radiant glow of these lanterns. Streets and homes are adorned with these vibrant symbols, creating a visual spectacle that transcends the practicality of illumination—it is a cultural manifestation of driving away darkness and inviting good fortune.

In the chapters that follow, we will delve into the significance of these New Year's Eve festivities, exploring the stories, symbolism, and cultural intricacies that make the transition from the old year to the new a momentous and joyous occasion. The collective spirit of celebration, rooted in age-old traditions, becomes a bridge connecting generations, communities, and the shared aspirations for a year filled with prosperity, happiness, and good fortune.

Customs for Luck and Prosperity

As the tapestry of Chinese New Year unfolds, intricately woven into the fabric of traditions are customs deeply rooted in the pursuit of luck and prosperity. These customs, handed down through generations, are more than mere rituals—they are sacred acts believed to invite positive energies, ward off misfortune, and ensure a year filled with abundance. In this chapter, we delve into the rich tapestry of customs that color the Chinese New Year celebration, exploring the significance, symbolism, and enduring legacy of practices aimed at ushering in good fortune.

Warding Off the Nian Monster:

The mythical Nian monster, whose presence once struck fear into the hearts of ancient villagers, continues to influence customs designed to repel its malevolent spirit. The loud crackling of firecrackers and the rhythmic beats of drums are not merely auditory spectacles—they are time-honored traditions believed to scare away the Nian, ensuring its retreat and the protection of homes and communities. The vibrant explosions of red fireworks are not just a visual delight; they are a symbolic act of banishing darkness and inviting prosperity.

Decorative Symbols for Prosperity:

Beyond the spectacle of fireworks, Chinese New Year is marked by the deliberate use of symbols and decorations believed to attract good fortune. The character "Fu," meaning good fortune, is often prominently displayed. Upside-down "Fu" characters, signifying the arrival of prosperity, are a common sight. The "Chunlian" or door couplets, poetic phrases laden with positive wishes, adorn entrances, infusing homes with auspicious energies. The meticulous placement of these symbols is not a mere aesthetic choice; it is a deliberate invocation of prosperity and joy.

Red Packets and Symbolic Numbers:

Red envelopes, or "Hongbao," exchanged during Chinese New Year are more than monetary gifts—they are symbolic gestures of goodwill and blessings. The act of giving and receiving Hongbao transcends the exchange of money; it is a tradition rooted in the belief that the transfer of wealth brings not only financial prosperity but also the well-wishes of the giver. The amounts, often containing even numbers, are chosen for their auspicious associations. Even numbers, believed to bring balance and harmony, are favored, while odd numbers are avoided, as they are associated with misfortune.

Offerings to Ancestors for Blessings:

The act of making offerings to ancestors during Chinese New Year is a poignant custom with deep cultural and spiritual significance. Families pay respects to their forebears, expressing gratitude for their wisdom and sacrifices. Offerings of food, tea, and other items are presented on ancestral altars, symbolizing a connection between the living and the departed. This ritual, known as "Bai Bai," seeks blessings from ancestors for health, prosperity, and harmony in the coming year.

Auspicious Food for Abundance:

The Reunion Dinner, a hallmark of Chinese New Year's Eve, is not only a culinary feast but a carefully orchestrated selection of dishes imbued with symbolism. Dumplings, resembling ancient Chinese gold and silver ingots, represent wealth and prosperity. Fish, with its association with surplus and abundance, is a staple on the New Year's Eve table. The circular shape of certain dishes symbolizes completeness and unity within the family. Each dish is chosen for its auspicious connotations, transforming the act of dining into a ritual of inviting prosperity and good fortune.

Dragon and Lion Dances: Symbolic Dance of Prosperity:

The iconic Dragon and Lion dances are integral to Chinese New Year celebrations, representing not only cultural vibrancy but also powerful symbols of luck and prosperity. The Dragon, a mythical creature associated with strength and good fortune, weaves through the streets, its undulating movements believed to bring rain—a symbol of abundance. The Lion dance, with its playful antics, is a spirited performance meant to chase away evil spirits and invite prosperity. These dynamic dances, accompanied by the rhythmic beats of drums and cymbals, infuse the atmosphere with positive energy.

The Tradition of First Footing: Bringing Good Fortune:

The concept of "First Footing" is a charming tradition observed in various regions, where the first person to enter a home after midnight on New Year's Eve is believed to bring good fortune for the coming year. The chosen individual, known as the "First Footer," is often selected for their positive energy and auspicious characteristics. The act of First Footing is not merely a symbolic gesture; it is a lively and joyous custom that embodies the spirit of welcoming good fortune into the household.

Plants and Flowers for Prosperity:

The careful selection and placement of plants and flowers during Chinese New Year are customs deeply intertwined with the pursuit of prosperity. Plum blossoms symbolize resilience and perseverance, while peonies represent wealth and prosperity. Tangerine trees, believed to bring good luck and fortune, are commonly displayed in homes and public spaces. Orchids, with their association with refinement and beauty, are also favored. These floral arrangements are not only visual embellishments; they are living symbols believed to attract positive energies.

The Significance of Cleaning: Sweeping Away Misfortune:

The act of spring cleaning before Chinese New Year is more than a routine of tidying up—it is a deliberate effort to sweep away the misfortunes of the past year and make way for the fresh energy of the new. Dust is swept away, windows are opened to allow stagnant energies to escape, and homes are meticulously cleaned in a symbolic act of inviting good luck. The practice of cleaning extends beyond the physical space to spiritual and emotional realms, creating a sense of renewal.

In the chapters that follow, we will delve deeper into the tapestry of customs for luck and prosperity, exploring the stories, symbolism, and cultural intricacies that make each practice a cherished part of Chinese New Year celebrations. These customs, passed down through generations, are not merely rituals; they are expressions of hope, unity, and the enduring belief in the possibility of a year filled with abundance and positive energies.

Chapter 2: Japanese New Year
Oshogatsu Traditions

In the Land of the Rising Sun, the arrival of the new year is not just a transition in the calendar; it is a cultural and spiritual journey woven with time-honored traditions. Oshogatsu, or Japanese New Year, is a tapestry of customs that reflect the deep-rooted values of the Japanese people—harmony, respect, purity, and a seamless blending of ancient traditions with contemporary celebrations. In this chapter, we delve into the rich and nuanced Oshogatsu traditions, exploring the meticulous preparations, symbolic rituals, and the profound sense of renewal that defines this auspicious time.

Joya No Kane: Welcoming the New Year with Temple Bells:

As the last hours of the year wane, Japan prepares for the timeless tradition of Joya No Kane, the ringing of temple bells. On New Year's Eve, Buddhist temples across the country toll their bells 108 times, a symbolic number representing the 108 worldly desires in Buddhist belief. The resonant sound reverberates through the crisp night air, dispelling the troubles of the past year and purifying the soul. Families often visit local temples to participate in this ritual, seeking spiritual renewal and a fresh start in the new year.

Hatsumode: The First Shrine Visit of the Year:

One of the most cherished Oshogatsu traditions is Hatsumode, the first shrine visit of the year. In the early days of January, people flock to Shinto shrines to offer prayers, seek blessings, and express gratitude for the past year. The act of Hatsumode is not only a religious observance but a communal event, as families and friends come together to usher in the new year with a spirit of unity and hope. The vibrant atmosphere around shrines, adorned with festive decorations, captures the essence of Oshogatsu.

Kadomatsu and Shimenawa: Symbolic Decorations:

The visual landscape of Oshogatsu is adorned with symbolic decorations, each carrying deep cultural meaning. Kadomatsu, or gate pine, is a traditional arrangement of pine branches, bamboo, and plum blossoms, carefully crafted to symbolize longevity, strength, and prosperity. Shimenawa, sacred Shinto rope, is draped around entrances and sacred spaces, signifying the boundary between the divine and the ordinary. These decorations not only add a visual charm to the festive season but also serve as visual expressions of cultural values and hopes for the coming year.

Osechi Ryori: Culinary Artistry for Prosperity:

The Oshogatsu feast, known as Osechi Ryori, is a culinary celebration that transcends mere sustenance. It is a meticulous art form, with each dish chosen for its auspicious symbolism and flavors. Traditional bento boxes, or jubako, are filled with an array of dishes, each carrying wishes for health, happiness, and prosperity. Black beans symbolize diligence, fish roe represents fertility, and sweet chestnuts embody family unity. The act of sharing Osechi Ryori with loved ones is not just a gastronomic experience; it is a communal expression of hope for a bountiful and harmonious year.

Toshikoshi Soba: Noodles for Longevity:

On the eve of the new year, it is customary to partake in toshikoshi soba, buckwheat noodles eaten for longevity. The act of consuming these long, uncut noodles symbolizes the desire for a long and prosperous life. The simplicity of the dish reflects the Japanese appreciation for the purity and beauty in the transient nature of life. Families come together to share this symbolic meal, fostering a sense of togetherness and gratitude for the passing year.

Otoshidama: Monetary Gifts for Good Luck:

A cherished tradition during Oshogatsu is the custom of giving and receiving Otoshidama, monetary gifts often presented in decorative envelopes. Elders gift these envelopes to younger family members, symbolizing good luck, prosperity, and blessings for the coming year. The act of receiving Otoshidama is not merely a financial transaction; it is a gesture of goodwill, fostering a sense of interconnectedness and mutual care within the family.

New Year's Greetings and Well-Wishing:

Oshogatsu is a time of heartfelt greetings and well-wishing, expressed through the exchange of New Year's cards known as Nengajo. These cards often feature the zodiac animal of the coming year, along with images of traditional symbols and scenes. The act of sending and receiving Nengajo is a thoughtful way to connect with friends, family, and colleagues, spreading warmth and good wishes for the new year.

Watching the First Sunrise:

Greeting the first sunrise of the year, known as Hatsuhinode, is a tradition rooted in the belief that the first light brings blessings and good fortune. Families often ascend to vantage points or coastal areas to witness this spectacular moment, symbolizing the hope for a bright and positive year ahead. The act of watching the first sunrise is not only a visual spectacle but a communal expression of optimism and unity.

Kagami Mochi and Mochitsuki: Celebrating with Rice Cakes:

Kagami Mochi, a traditional display of stacked rice cakes, is a symbolic representation of Oshogatsu. The two-tiered arrangement, topped with a bitter orange (daidai) or a leafy citrus fruit, signifies longevity and the passing of generations. Mochitsuki, the practice of pounding rice to make mochi (rice cakes), is a communal event where families and communities come together to participate in the rhythmic and celebratory process. Mochi, with its soft and sticky texture, symbolizes the hope for a harmonious and close-knit community.

Joyano Kane: Evening Bell Ringing for Happiness:

On New Year's Eve, as the sun sets and the world awaits the stroke of midnight, some communities partake in the tradition of Joyano Kane, the ringing of bells at local temples. This rhythmic ringing, typically performed 108 times, echoes the Buddhist belief in purifying the 108 earthly desires. The resonance of the bells symbolizes the dispelling of impurities and the invitation of happiness in the new year.

In the chapters that follow, we will explore these Oshogatsu traditions in greater detail, unraveling the stories, symbolism, and cultural nuances that make Japanese New Year a celebration rich in spiritual depth and communal resonance. Oshogatsu is not merely a passage of time; it is a cultural symphony, where traditions, both ancient and contemporary, converge to create a tapestry of renewal, harmony, and shared aspirations for the unfolding year.

Hatsumode Temple Visits

In the tranquil landscapes of Japan, where the intersection of spirituality and cultural traditions is seamless, the practice of Hatsumode stands as a beacon, signaling the beginning of a new year filled with hope, reflection, and collective aspirations. Hatsumode, the first shrine visit of the year, is a sacred journey undertaken by millions across the country, embodying the essence of Oshogatsu—the Japanese New Year. As we embark on this exploration of Hatsumode, we delve into the profound significance, rituals, and communal spirit that define this timeless tradition.

The Spiritual Pilgrimage:

As the calendar turns its pages and the first rays of sunlight illuminate the horizon on New Year's Day, Japan is awakened to the resonance of Hatsumode—a spiritual pilgrimage that beckons individuals, families, and communities to Shinto shrines nationwide. The term "Hatsumode" translates to "the first visit," symbolizing the inaugural steps into the sacred realm of the shrine to seek blessings, express gratitude, and set the tone for the coming year. It is a journey steeped in spirituality, cultural reverence, and a deep sense of connection to both the divine and the collective spirit of the Japanese people.

Preparations and Anticipation:

In the days leading up to the new year, a palpable sense of anticipation pervades the air as individuals and families prepare for Hatsumode. The meticulous cleaning of homes, selection of traditional attire, and thoughtful consideration of prayers and wishes become integral aspects of the preparations. Families gather, generations intertwining, as they embark on this collective journey to shrines, marking the beginning of the year with a tapestry of shared hopes and aspirations.

Choosing the Right Shrine:

While Hatsumode is practiced across Shinto shrines throughout Japan, there are certain shrines that hold particular significance and draw larger crowds. Meiji Shrine in Tokyo, Fushimi Inari Taisha in Kyoto, and Atsuta Shrine in Nagoya are among the notable destinations where pilgrims gather to partake in the rituals. The choice of shrine often reflects personal beliefs, regional traditions, or a connection to specific deities associated with the desired blessings.

Midnight Visits and Countdowns:

Hatsumode is not confined to daylight hours; it extends into the midnight moments that mark the transition from the old year to the new. Many shrines open their gates at the stroke of midnight, and worshippers, clad in traditional attire or contemporary clothing, gather to make their initial prayers as the year unfolds. Temples across Japan host countdown events, blending the spiritual with the celebratory as people await the ringing of bells and the symbolic entry into the new year.

Embracing Tradition in Modern Times:

While Hatsumode is rooted in centuries-old traditions, it seamlessly integrates into the fabric of modern life. The experience of Hatsumode has evolved to accommodate contemporary sensibilities, with some shrines employing technology to enhance the pilgrim's journey. Digital offerings, interactive displays, and online reservations have become part of the Hatsumode experience, bridging the ancient and the modern in a harmonious blend.

Purification Rites: Temizu and Chozuya:

The journey into the sacred space of the shrine begins with purification rites, emphasizing the importance of spiritual cleanliness. Worshippers approach temizuya, a water pavilion often situated near the shrine's entrance, where they perform ritualistic cleansing. Using a ladle, individuals wash their hands and mouths, symbolizing the purification of the body and soul before entering the sacred precincts. The act of purification, known as "misogi," is a symbolic transition from the mundane to the sacred.

Omamori: Sacred Talismans for Protection:

Central to Hatsumode is the acquisition of omamori, sacred talismans or amulets believed to bestow protection, good fortune, and specific blessings. Pilgrims visit stalls or designated areas within the shrine where they can purchase omamori, each designed for a particular purpose—safe travels, academic success, health, or general well-being. These intricately crafted talismans become tangible reminders of the divine blessings sought during Hatsumode, often carried throughout the year for spiritual reassurance.

Ema: Wooden Wishes Hung with Hope:

Ema, small wooden plaques, play a significant role in Hatsumode. Pilgrims purchase ema from the shrine, inscribing their wishes and prayers on the wooden surface. These ema are then hung on designated racks within the shrine, forming a collective tapestry of aspirations. The act of hanging an ema is a personal and communal gesture, intertwining individual hopes with the collective wish for a harmonious and prosperous year.

New Year's Prayers: Rituals of Expression:

The heart of Hatsumode lies in the prayers offered at the main hall of the shrine. Pilgrims approach the haiden, the worship hall, where they present their prayers, wishes, and expressions of gratitude to the kami, the Shinto deities. The ringing of the shrine bell, the bowing of heads, and the symbolic offering of coins all contribute to the sacred exchange between the worshipper and the divine. The atmosphere is imbued with a sense of reverence and sincerity as individuals articulate their hopes for health, success, and happiness in the coming year.

O-Nenjitsu: New Year's Celebration within the Shrine:

Hatsumode extends beyond the rituals of prayer; it encompasses a celebration within the sacred confines of the shrine. Festive activities, performances, and cultural events are often organized as part of O-Nenjitsu, the New Year's celebration. Traditional music, dance, and processions create a vibrant ambiance, fostering a sense of community and joy among worshippers. The shrine becomes a focal point for cultural exchange, bridging generations and reinforcing the bonds that tie the community together.

Fortune-telling: Omikuji and Hamaya:

A visit to the shrine during Hatsumode often includes the practice of omikuji, a form of fortune-telling. Pilgrims draw paper strips containing predictions ranging from great fortune to potential challenges. Depending on the prediction, individuals may choose to tie the omikuji to designated racks within the shrine, leaving the fortune in the hands of fate. Additionally, hamaya, arrow-shaped amulets believed to ward off evil spirits and bring good fortune, are popular items acquired during Hatsumode.

Goshuin: Sacred Shrine Seal as a Memento:

Goshuin, sacred shrine seals, serve as cherished mementos of Hatsumode. Pilgrims present their goshuincho, a special book for collecting shrine seals, to the shrine priest. In return, the priest inscribes the goshuin with intricate calligraphy and stamps it with the shrine's unique seal. Each goshuin is a testament to the pilgrim's spiritual journey, a tangible record of their visit to the sacred space.

The Social Aspect: Community and Togetherness:

Hatsumode is not solely an individual or familial undertaking; it is a communal experience that fosters a profound sense of togetherness. Families, friends, and even strangers come together in the shared pursuit of spiritual blessings and cultural reverence. The queues that form outside popular shrines become avenues for conversations, shared excitement, and a collective acknowledgment of the significance of the moment. Hatsumode, in this communal context, becomes a celebration of unity and the shared journey into the new year.

Contemporary Innovations:

In contemporary Japan, Hatsumode has evolved to embrace technological innovations while preserving its core traditions. Some shrines offer online reservations to manage crowd sizes, and virtual Hatsumode experiences have been developed to accommodate those unable to visit in person. The integration of modern conveniences harmonizes with the timeless essence of Hatsumode, ensuring that the tradition remains accessible and meaningful in a changing world.

In the chapters that follow, we will continue our exploration of Oshogatsu traditions, unraveling the stories, symbolism, and cultural nuances that make Japanese New Year a celebration that transcends time and resonates with the spirit of renewal and collective aspirations. Hatsumode, with its rich tapestry of rituals and community spirit, serves as a testament to the enduring cultural legacy that defines the beginning of each new year in Japan.

Lucky Foods

In the kaleidoscope of Oshogatsu traditions, where each ritual and symbol weaves a tapestry of cultural significance, the culinary landscape stands as a vibrant and essential thread. Lucky foods during Japanese New Year, or Oshogatsu, are not merely sustenance; they are edible symbols infused with centuries of tradition, beliefs, and the collective wish for prosperity, health, and joy in the coming year. As we embark on this culinary journey, we explore the rich palette of flavors, symbolism, and cultural nuances that define the lucky foods of Oshogatsu.

Sekihan: Red Rice for Celebration:

At the heart of Oshogatsu feasts is Sekihan, a dish that radiates both festive colors and cultural significance. This dish, featuring glutinous rice steamed with azuki beans, transforms into a vibrant shade of red—a color symbolizing celebration, happiness, and the warding off of evil spirits. Sekihan is often reserved for special occasions, and its presence during Oshogatsu marks the importance of the moment and the wish for a joyous year ahead.

Ozoni: Soup of Good Fortune:

Ozoni, a traditional soup featuring mochi (rice cake) and various ingredients in a clear or miso-based broth, is a quintessential dish enjoyed on New Year's Day. The preparation of Ozoni varies across regions and households, with ingredients such as chicken, fish, vegetables, and yuzu peel contributing to the diverse flavors of this comforting soup. The round shape of mochi symbolizes harmony, and consuming Ozoni is believed to bring good fortune and smooth transitions in the coming year.

Kuromame: Sweet Black Soybeans for Health:

Kuromame, sweet black soybeans simmered in sugar and soy sauce, are a staple of Oshogatsu cuisine. The glossy, black hue of these beans is associated with health and the warding off of evil spirits. The natural sweetness of kuromame adds a delightful contrast to the savory and umami flavors present in the overall Oshogatsu menu. In many households, kuromame is prepared in abundance, symbolizing a wish for a sweet and healthy life.

Kazunoko: Herring Roe for Prosperity:

Kazunoko, or herring roe, is a delicacy associated with fertility and prosperity. The tiny, golden orbs are reminiscent of abundance and fertility, making them a symbolic inclusion in Oshogatsu feasts. The dish is often marinated in a soy-based sauce, imparting a savory flavor that complements the overall diversity of flavors on the New Year's table. The consumption of kazunoko expresses the collective wish for prosperity, growth, and abundance in the coming year.

Tai: Sea Bream for Good Fortune:

Tai, or sea bream, holds a special place in Oshogatsu celebrations as a harbinger of good fortune. The pronunciation of "tai" in Japanese is similar to the word for "medetai," meaning joyous or auspicious. As a result, tai is often served as a whole fish, symbolizing completeness and the wish for a year filled with happiness. The vibrant red color of tai further enhances its symbolism, representing vitality, energy, and good health.

Kohaku Namasu: Shredded Vegetables for Joy:

Kohaku Namasu, a refreshing salad of shredded daikon radish and carrot, is not only a colorful addition to the Oshogatsu table but also a symbol of joy and celebration. The combination of white and orange hues in kohaku namasu represents purity and happiness. The ingredients are marinated in a mixture of rice vinegar, sugar, and salt, creating a crisp and flavorful dish that serves as a palate cleanser and a visual delight.

Kamaboko: Steamed Fish Cake for Longevity:

Kamaboko, a steamed fish cake often sliced into festive patterns, holds significance as a symbol of longevity. The Japanese believe that the fish cake's firm and resilient texture mirrors the qualities of a long and prosperous life. The bright colors and decorative patterns of kamaboko add visual appeal to Oshogatsu dishes, enhancing the overall aesthetic of the New Year's feast.

Ebi: Shrimp for a Long Life:

Ebi, or shrimp, is another auspicious ingredient that finds its way onto Oshogatsu tables. The curvature of the shrimp is symbolic of a long and healthy life, and its inclusion in dishes such as sushi or sashimi expresses the wish for longevity. The vibrant color and succulent texture of ebi contribute to the overall sensory experience of Oshogatsu cuisine.

Nishime: Simmered Vegetables for Harmony:

Nishime, a dish of simmered vegetables and meat, embodies the spirit of harmony and unity. The assortment of ingredients, including root vegetables like carrots and lotus root, is carefully prepared and cooked in a flavorful broth. The slow simmering process allows the flavors to meld, creating a dish that represents the coming together of diverse elements in a harmonious blend. Nishime is often served in generous portions, symbolizing abundance and the shared joys of communal living.

Toso: Sweet Sake for Good Health:

Toso, a sweet sake infused with medicinal herbs, is a traditional New Year's drink believed to promote good health. The preparation of toso often involves a family ritual, with each member taking turns to participate in the process. The consumption of toso during Oshogatsu is seen as a proactive measure to ward off illness and ensure well-being in the coming year. The shared act of raising a cup of toso is also a symbolic gesture of collective health and happiness.

Datemaki: Sweet Rolled Omelet for Knowledge:

Datemaki, a sweet rolled omelet, is a dish associated with the pursuit of knowledge and scholarship. The layered, rolled structure of datemaki resembles a scroll, symbolizing the pages of a book. As such, the inclusion of datemaki in Oshogatsu cuisine expresses the wish for academic success, intellectual growth, and the acquisition of knowledge in the coming year.

Zoni: Regional Variations and Personal Touches:

While certain dishes like ozoni and sekihan are commonly enjoyed across Japan, Oshogatsu cuisine also embraces regional variations and personal touches. Each household may have its unique spin on traditional recipes, incorporating local ingredients, family traditions, and culinary innovations. The diversity of Oshogatsu dishes reflects the rich cultural tapestry of Japan, where culinary expressions intertwine with individual and regional identities.

Sweet Endings: Kagami Mochi and Oshiruko:

As Oshogatsu festivities reach their culinary crescendo, sweet endings become a focal point. Kagami Mochi, the decorative display of stacked rice cakes, serves both as a visual centerpiece and a delicious treat. The round shape of the mochi symbolizes completeness and unity, while the traditional offering of this sweet confection signifies the wish for a harmonious and fulfilling year.

Oshiruko, a sweet red bean soup often served with mochi or grilled rice cakes, provides a warm and comforting conclusion to the Oshogatsu feast. The sweetness of the red bean soup and the chewy texture of mochi combine to create a delightful sensory experience, marking the conclusion of the New Year's culinary celebration.

In the chapters that follow, we will continue our exploration of Oshogatsu traditions, unraveling the stories, symbolism, and cultural nuances that make Japanese New Year a celebration that engages not only the spirit but also the senses. Lucky foods, with their vibrant flavors and symbolic significance, serve as both nourishment for the body and expressions of collective wishes for prosperity, health, and joy in the unfolding year.

Joya No Kane: Bell Ringing for Reflection and Renewal

In the quietude of the Japanese night, as the old year bids its farewell and the first whispers of the new year beckon, the air resonates with the timeless tradition of Joya No Kane—the rhythmic tolling of temple bells. This ancient practice, observed on New Year's Eve, transcends the boundaries of time, inviting worshippers and onlookers alike to participate in a profound ritual of reflection, purification, and the collective aspiration for renewal. As we explore the intricate layers of Joya No Kane, we delve into the spiritual resonance, cultural significance, and communal spirit that make this bell ringing ceremony an integral part of Oshogatsu, the Japanese New Year.

The Origin and Essence of Joya No Kane:

Joya No Kane, which translates to "ringing of the bells on New Year's Eve," is a practice deeply rooted in Buddhist tradition. The origins of this ritual can be traced back over a millennium to ancient China, where the custom of ringing bells on New Year's Eve was believed to expel the troubles of the past year and welcome the purity of the new. This tradition found its way to Japan, evolving into the intricate ceremony we know today.

The essence of Joya No Kane extends beyond a mere auditory spectacle; it is a spiritual journey marking the passage of time, the purification of the soul, and the collective aspiration for a fresh start. The rhythmic tolling of the temple bells is believed to reach every corner of existence, dispelling impurities, negativities, and ill fortunes, creating a sacred space for the dawn of a new beginning.

The Symbolic Number 108:

At the heart of Joya No Kane is the symbolic number 108, a figure deeply ingrained in Buddhist philosophy. According to Buddhist belief, humans are bound by 108 earthly desires or "bonno," which encompass a range of attachments, cravings, and delusions. The ringing of the temple bells 108 times on New Year's Eve is a ritualistic purification, symbolizing the dispelling of these desires and the journey toward enlightenment.

The resonance of each toll is considered a symbolic cleansing, inviting worshippers to reflect on the attachments and distractions that bind them to the mundane world. As the tolls echo through the night, it is believed that the vibrations reach the heavens, purifying both the individual and the collective consciousness.

Temple Selection and Community Gatherings:

Joya No Kane is observed in Buddhist temples across Japan, each with its unique charm and significance. While major temples in urban centers draw large crowds, even smaller local temples become focal points for the community's observance of this sacred tradition. The choice of temple may be influenced by personal beliefs, familial traditions, or the spiritual resonance one feels with a particular sacred space.

In the lead-up to New Year's Eve, communities come together to prepare for Joya No Kane. Temples organize special events, workshops, and gatherings that not only guide worshippers in the proper observance of the ritual but also foster a sense of community and shared purpose. Families, friends, and neighbors often join in this collective preparation, deepening the bonds that tie them to both the spiritual and human realms.

Attire and Symbolic Items:

As worshippers make their way to the temple to participate in Joya No Kane, attire plays a significant role in enhancing the ritual's spiritual ambiance. Many choose to wear traditional Japanese garments, such as kimono or hakama, symbolizing reverence and respect for the sacred occasion. The act of donning these traditional attires is not merely a nod to cultural heritage; it is a conscious effort to approach the ceremony with a sense of solemnity and cultural continuity.

In addition to traditional attire, participants often carry symbolic items. Omamori, protective amulets, may be clutched in hands, offering a tangible connection to the spiritual realm. Candles and incense, with their symbolic roles in purification and offering, become integral elements of the Joya No Kane ceremony, heightening the sensory experience and connecting participants to the ancient traditions they are about to partake in.

Timing and Preparation for the Ceremony:

As the sun dips below the horizon on New Year's Eve, casting a hushed glow over the landscape, the anticipation for Joya No Kane builds. Temples prepare for the ceremony by ensuring that the temple bells are in optimal condition, with some even enlisting skilled craftsmen to fine-tune the resonance. The atmosphere within the temple becomes charged with a palpable sense of expectation, as worshippers gather to usher in the new year with a ceremony that transcends the boundaries of time.

The timing of Joya No Kane is meticulous, with the first tolls usually commencing shortly before midnight. The intervals between tolls allow worshippers to reflect, to meditate, and to absorb the spiritual energy unfolding with each resonant echo. Temples often provide guidance on the proper posture and mindset for participants, creating an environment conducive to introspection and communion with the sacred.

The Reverberating Sound:

The tolling of the temple bells during Joya No Kane is not a hurried or chaotic affair. Each toll is deliberate, measured, and imbued with a profound sense of purpose. The resonant sound unfolds like a meditative melody, echoing through the temple precincts and beyond, permeating the night with a sacred vibration.

The sound of the bells is believed to resonate with the vibrations of the universe, creating a harmonious alignment between the individual and the cosmos. Participants often close their eyes, allowing the sound to envelop them, transcending the physical realm and connecting with the spiritual essence of the ceremony. It is a moment of deep introspection, where the past is released, and the slate is wiped clean for the coming year.

Personal Reflection and Aspiration:

Joya No Kane is not a passive observance; it is a participatory ritual that invites worshippers to engage in personal reflection and aspiration. As the bells toll, individuals contemplate the experiences, challenges, and lessons of the past year. It is a time to acknowledge achievements, express gratitude, and release attachments that may hinder spiritual growth.

Worshippers also use this sacred moment to set intentions for the coming year. The vibrations of the bells are believed to carry these aspirations into the universe, acting as a conduit for the individual's wishes to reach the divine realm. It is a deeply personal and yet collective act, where individuals stand together in their shared humanity, bound by a common desire for renewal and spiritual growth.

The Collective Resonance:

Joya No Kane is not confined to the temple grounds; it resonates with a collective spirit that extends far beyond the physical boundaries of the ceremony. Across cities and villages, the sound of temple bells mingles with the stillness of the night, creating a collective resonance that unites communities in a shared moment of reflection and renewal.

Families, friends, and neighbors, whether physically present at the temple or hearing the distant tolls from their homes, become part of a larger tapestry of shared experience. The collective resonance of Joya No Kane serves as a reminder that, despite the diversity of individual journeys, there is a shared thread that binds humanity in its quest for spiritual connection and renewal.

After the Toll: Welcoming the New Year:

As the last toll of Joya No Kane reverberates through the night, the transition into the new year is marked. Temples often host additional rituals and ceremonies to welcome worshippers into the first moments of the year, further reinforcing the sense of spiritual communion and renewal. Participants may engage in prayers, chants, or silent meditation, creating a seamless transition from the bell-ringing ceremony to the unfolding possibilities of the new year.

Many temples also offer symbolic items and charms for worshippers to take home, serving as tangible reminders of the spiritual journey undertaken during Joya No Kane. These items, whether omamori, blessed sake, or written prayers, become cherished artifacts that carry the energy of the ceremony into the daily lives of the participants.

Contemporary Adaptations and Innovations:

In the contemporary landscape, Joya No Kane has adapted to meet the needs and preferences of diverse communities. Some temples offer live-streamed or virtual Joya No Kane experiences, allowing worshippers to participate from the comfort of their homes. Digital platforms and social media have become avenues for sharing the spiritual essence of Joya No Kane with a global audience, fostering a sense of connection and unity beyond physical boundaries.

Additionally, there has been a revival of interest in Joya No Kane among younger generations. Temples and cultural organizations are exploring creative ways to engage the youth in the ancient traditions, integrating modern elements such as multimedia presentations, interactive workshops, and community events. This dynamic approach ensures that the spirit of Joya No Kane continues to resonate with evolving sensibilities, bridging the gap between tradition and contemporary expression.

Joya No Kane and the Journey Within:

At its core, Joya No Kane is more than a cultural ritual or a religious observance; it is a journey within—the tolling of the bells becomes a meditative guide, leading participants into the depths of self-reflection and spiritual renewal. In the quietude of the temple, as the echoes of the bells fade into the night, individuals emerge with a heightened sense of clarity, purpose, and connection to the vast tapestry of existence.

Joya No Kane invites us to embrace the cyclical nature of time, recognizing that each toll carries with it the echoes of countless generations who have participated in this ritual. It is a moment of transcendence, where the past dissolves, the present is illuminated, and the future unfolds with infinite possibilities. The collective journey of Joya No Kane is a testament to the enduring power of ritual, community, and the timeless quest for spiritual growth.

As we continue our exploration of Oshogatsu traditions in the chapters that follow, the echoes of Joya No Kane linger—a reminder that in the stillness of reflection, the soul finds its resonance, and in the tolling of the bells, the spirit embarks on an eternal journey of renewal and rebirth.

Chapter 3: Rosh Hashanah
Sweet Symbolism

In the rich tapestry of Jewish tradition, Rosh Hashanah, the Jewish New Year, unfolds with a symphony of symbolic rituals and meaningful customs. At the heart of these traditions lies a profound appreciation for the symbolic power of sweetness, where every bite becomes a metaphor, and every dish becomes a vessel for expressing hopes, aspirations, and a collective yearning for a sweet and fruitful year ahead. As we explore the sweet symbolism of Rosh Hashanah, we delve into the significance of honey, apples, and other delectable delights that grace the festive table, carrying with them the weight of centuries of tradition and the promise of a new beginning.

Honey: The Golden Nectar of Renewal:

At the center of Rosh Hashanah's sweet symbolism is honey, a golden elixir that transcends its culinary role to become a metaphor for the sweetness of life, the promise of renewal, and the hope for a year filled with blessings. The tradition of dipping apples in honey, a ubiquitous practice during Rosh Hashanah, serves as a poignant expression of these sentiments.

As families gather around the festive table, a bowl of golden honey takes its place alongside ripe, crisp apples. The act of dipping the apple into honey and partaking in its sweetness becomes a ritualistic gesture, symbolizing the collective wish for a year that overflows with the goodness and sweetness of life. The apple, representing the cycle of life and nature's bounty, becomes a vessel for the transformative power of honey—a tangible reminder that even in the face of challenges, there is the potential for sweetness and renewal.

Apples: Symbolism of Continuity and Wholeness:

Beyond their role in the honey-dipping ritual, apples bear their own symbolism in the context of Rosh Hashanah. The roundness of the apple, without a beginning or an end, mirrors the cyclical nature of time and the continuity of life. As the shofar sounds and prayers resonate, the apple serves as a visual metaphor for the eternal cycle of creation, reflection, and renewal that defines Rosh Hashanah.

In Jewish tradition, the apple tree is also associated with the Garden of Eden, further enhancing the symbolism of apples during Rosh Hashanah. The connection to Eden reinforces the theme of renewal and the aspiration to return to a state of spiritual wholeness. As each bite is taken, the crisp texture and natural sweetness of the apple become a reminder of the potential for personal growth and the pursuit of a life lived in harmony with one's beliefs.

Challah: Braided Bread of Unity:

Challah, the traditional braided bread, graces the Rosh Hashanah table with its golden crust and soft interior, symbolizing the interconnectedness of life and the unity of the Jewish community. The braided shape, with its multiple strands woven together, represents the bonds that tie individuals, families, and the entire Jewish people in a shared journey of faith and tradition.

During Rosh Hashanah, it is customary to elevate the symbolism of challah by incorporating sweet ingredients such as honey and raisins. The addition of sweetness to the bread echoes the overarching theme of the holiday—a desire for a year filled with blessings and joy. As families gather to break bread, the act becomes more than a shared meal; it is a communal expression of unity, continuity, and the shared aspirations for sweetness in the coming year.

Pomegranate: Seeds of Prosperity and Good Deeds:

The pomegranate, with its vibrant ruby-red seeds, holds a special place in the symbolism of Rosh Hashanah. In Jewish tradition, the pomegranate is associated with abundance, fertility, and prosperity. Its many seeds, tightly packed within the fruit, are seen as symbols of the numerous good deeds that one can perform in the coming year. As the pomegranate is opened and its seeds revealed, it becomes a visual representation of the potential for a year filled with acts of kindness, generosity, and prosperity.

The custom of eating pomegranate seeds during Rosh Hashanah is a tangible way of expressing the collective desire for a fruitful and fulfilling year. The burst of flavor from each seed is a reminder that, much like the pomegranate, life is full of hidden treasures waiting to be discovered. As families share the seeds, they share in the hope for a year abundant in both tangible and intangible blessings.

Dates: Symbol of a Sweet and Timely Year:

Dates, with their natural sweetness and rich symbolism, find a place on the Rosh Hashanah table as a representation of the desire for a year filled with sweetness and well-timed opportunities. In Hebrew, the word for date, "tamar," is associated with the concept of ending and completing a cycle. As Rosh Hashanah marks the conclusion of one year and the beginning of another, the inclusion of dates becomes a metaphor for the timely and sweet moments that define our lives.

As families partake in the ritual of eating dates, the act becomes a shared acknowledgement of the cyclical nature of time and the potential for sweet endings and new beginnings. Each bite serves as a reminder to savor the present moment and to approach the unfolding year with an appreciation for the sweetness it may bring.

Nuts and Seeds: A Wish for a Year of Prosperity:

The tradition of including a variety of nuts and seeds on the Rosh Hashanah table carries with it the symbolism of prosperity and the aspiration for a year filled with abundance. Almonds, with their rich flavor and textured exterior, are often featured, symbolizing fertility and the potential for new growth. Other nuts, such as walnuts and hazelnuts, contribute their own unique flavors and textures, creating a diverse and symbolic array.

The act of eating nuts and seeds becomes a gesture of solidarity with the collective wish for prosperity in the coming year. The crackling sound as shells are opened and the rich taste of the nuts represent the anticipation of breaking through barriers and experiencing the richness that life has to offer.

Honey Cake: A Culinary Tapestry of Sweetness:

No exploration of the sweet symbolism of Rosh Hashanah would be complete without a mention of honey cake. This moist and flavorful dessert, infused with the sweetness of honey, is a culinary centerpiece that encapsulates the essence of the holiday. The honey cake becomes a metaphor for the interconnectedness of tradition, family, and the sweetness of life itself.

The preparation of honey cake often involves the blending of diverse ingredients, each contributing its unique flavor and texture. Spices such as cinnamon and nutmeg add warmth, while nuts and dried fruits introduce layers of complexity. The act of baking honey cake becomes a familial tradition, with each generation contributing to the tapestry of flavors that define this symbolic dessert.

As families gather to enjoy a slice of honey cake, the act becomes a shared experience—a moment to savor the sweetness of tradition, the richness of family bonds, and the anticipation of a new year filled with the flavors of hope and joy.

Rituals and Blessings Around the Table:

The act of partaking in the sweet symbols of Rosh Hashanah extends beyond mere consumption; it becomes a series of rituals and blessings that enrich the experience and infuse it with deeper meaning. As the honey is dipped, the apples are crunched, and the various sweet delicacies are savored, families engage in a tapestry of rituals that connect them to the ancient traditions of the holiday.

Before partaking in the sweet offerings, families often recite blessings and prayers, expressing gratitude for the blessings of the past year and seeking divine favor for the year ahead. The act of sharing these blessings around the table creates a sacred space, where words of hope and aspiration blend with the aromas and flavors of the festive feast.

Contemporary Expressions of Sweet Symbolism:

In the contemporary landscape, the sweet symbolism of Rosh Hashanah has found new expressions and adaptations. Creative culinary interpretations, innovative recipes, and the use of locally sourced and seasonal ingredients have become integral to the modern celebration of the holiday. Families may experiment with new ways of incorporating sweetness into their Rosh Hashanah meals, embracing both tradition and innovation.

Additionally, the global interconnectedness facilitated by technology has allowed for the sharing of Rosh Hashanah traditions and recipes across diverse communities. Social media platforms, cooking blogs, and virtual gatherings have become avenues for individuals to connect, share, and celebrate the sweet symbolism of Rosh Hashanah in ways that resonate with their unique cultural and personal contexts.

Conclusion: A Tapestry of Sweetness and Hope:

As families come together to celebrate Rosh Hashanah, the sweet symbolism woven into the fabric of the holiday becomes a tapestry of shared experiences, hopes, and aspirations. The honey-dipped apples, the braided challah, the bursting pomegranate seeds, and the rich flavors of honey cake—all contribute to a sensory feast that transcends the boundaries of time and space.

In each bite, there is a collective acknowledgment of the sweetness that life offers, the continuity of tradition, and the potential for renewal. The symbolic foods of Rosh Hashanah serve as messengers, carrying the collective wishes and prayers of a community bound by faith, history, and a shared journey into the future.

As we delve into the chapters that follow, exploring the rich traditions of Rosh Hashanah, the sweet symbolism remains a guiding thread—a reminder that even in the symbolic act of eating, there is the potential for profound connection, gratitude, and the anticipation of a year filled with sweetness, joy, and the blessings of a new beginning.

High Holiday Rituals

As the sun sets, ushering in the sacred observance of Rosh Hashanah, the Jewish New Year, a profound tapestry of high holiday rituals unfolds. Rooted in centuries of tradition and guided by the spiritual significance of the occasion, these rituals become a means of connecting with the divine, reflecting on the past year, and embracing the potential for personal and communal renewal. In this exploration of Rosh Hashanah's high holiday rituals, we delve into the soul-stirring practices that define this period of introspection, repentance, and hopeful anticipation for the coming year.

Sound of the Shofar: A Call to Spiritual Awakening:

Central to the observance of Rosh Hashanah is the resounding blast of the shofar, a ceremonial ram's horn. The shofar's call echoes across synagogues and homes, serving as a primal and evocative sound that transcends language. The blowing of the shofar is not just a musical performance; it is a spiritual call to awaken the soul, stirring the depths of individual consciousness and inviting a collective response to the sacred season.

The shofar is blown in a series of distinctive sounds—Tekiah (a long, solid note), Shevarim (three broken, staccato notes), and Teruah (a series of short, rapid notes). Each sound carries its own symbolism, representing themes of completeness, brokenness, and alarm. The overarching message of the shofar's call is a call to teshuvah, or repentance—a return to one's true self and a reconnection with the divine.

Selichot Prayers: Prelude to Repentance:

In the days leading up to Rosh Hashanah, a special set of prayers known as Selichot is recited. These prayers serve as a prelude to the season of repentance, setting the spiritual tone for the High Holidays. The word "Selichot" is derived from the Hebrew root meaning forgiveness, reflecting the central theme of seeking divine pardon and reconciling with one's actions.

Selichot prayers often include poignant pleas for mercy, expressions of regret, and requests for divine understanding. The liturgy is crafted to inspire introspection and humility, creating a spiritual atmosphere that prepares individuals for the transformative journey of self-examination and repentance that defines the Rosh Hashanah season.

Tashlich: Casting Off Sins by the Water's Edge:

A distinctive and symbolic ritual observed during the Rosh Hashanah season is Tashlich, meaning "casting off" in Hebrew. This ritual takes place beside a body of flowing water, such as a river or stream, and involves the symbolic casting away of sins, regrets, and shortcomings. As individuals stand at the water's edge, they participate in a meditative process of introspection and release.

Traditionally, breadcrumbs or small pieces of bread are brought to the water, symbolizing the sins and transgressions of the past year. In a symbolic gesture, participants cast these crumbs into the flowing water, watching as the currents carry them away. The act is a tangible expression of the desire to unburden oneself from the weight of past mistakes and embark on the new year with a cleansed spirit.

Prayer Services: Amidst Melodies and Ancient Words:

The heart of Rosh Hashanah is found in the prayer services that fill synagogues with melodies, ancient words, and a palpable sense of spiritual energy. The liturgy of Rosh Hashanah prayers is infused with themes of divine kingship, judgment, and the universal hope for a year of sweetness and blessing. The prayer services are typically lengthier than usual, providing ample time for reflection, repentance, and the communal expression of shared aspirations.

The central prayer of Rosh Hashanah is the Amidah, which includes special blessings for the holiday. During this prayer, worshippers stand before the divine, expressing their desires for life, sustenance, and redemption in the coming year. The unique melodies and tunes associated with Rosh Hashanah prayers evoke a sense of solemnity and anticipation, creating an immersive and spiritually charged environment.

Kiddush and Festive Meals: Sanctifying the New Year:

Rosh Hashanah meals are infused with special rituals, beginning with the sanctification of the holiday through the recitation of Kiddush—the blessing over wine. The wine represents the joy and sanctity of the occasion, and the Kiddush is a proclamation of the holiness of the Jewish New Year. Families gather around the table, raising their glasses in unison, and ushering in the festive meals with expressions of gratitude and hope.

The festive meals themselves are a culmination of culinary traditions and symbolic foods, each bite infused with meaning and intention. The round challah, symbolizing the cyclical nature of life, takes its place alongside the honey-dipped apples, sweetening the anticipation for a year of blessings. As families partake in the festive meals, the act becomes a collective affirmation of faith, unity, and the shared journey into the new year.

Additional Customs: A Tapestry of Tradition:

Rosh Hashanah is woven with a tapestry of additional customs and practices, each contributing to the richness of the holiday observance. Some families have the custom of reciting Yehi Ratzon, a series of prayers and blessings that accompany the consumption of symbolic foods. Others incorporate the recitation of special psalms or engage in acts of charity as a means of expressing their commitment to righteousness and compassion in the coming year.

Many communities also engage in the creation of intricate Rosh Hashanah cards, sending wishes of sweetness, health, and prosperity to loved ones. The exchange of these cards becomes a modern expression of the timeless desire to connect, uplift, and share in the collective hopes for a better future.

Contemporary Expressions: Embracing Tradition in the Modern Era:

In the contemporary era, Rosh Hashanah rituals have found new expressions and adaptations that resonate with the dynamics of modern Jewish life. Digital platforms and virtual gatherings have become tools for fostering community engagement, allowing individuals to connect with prayer services, participate in communal rituals, and share in the joy of the holiday, even when physically distant.

Additionally, there is a growing movement towards environmentally conscious observance, with an emphasis on sustainability and eco-friendly practices. Some communities incorporate themes of environmental stewardship into their Tashlich rituals, using biodegradable materials for the symbolic casting off of sins.

Conclusion: A Spiritual Odyssey Unfolding:

As we conclude our exploration of the high holiday rituals of Rosh Hashanah, we recognize that this sacred season is not merely a series of observances; it is a spiritual odyssey unfolding across time and generations. The sound of the shofar, the resonance of prayers, the casting off of sins by the water's edge, and the shared meals—all contribute to a journey of introspection, repentance, and hopeful anticipation for the coming year.

In each ritual, there is an invitation to transcend the ordinary and connect with the eternal. Whether standing at the water's edge during Tashlich, reciting prayers within the hallowed walls of a synagogue, or raising a glass in Kiddush, individuals participate in a communal tapestry of tradition that links them to their ancestors and binds them to the collective destiny of the Jewish people.

As we move forward into the chapters that follow, exploring the depths of Rosh Hashanah's symbolism, history, and traditions, the echoes of these high holiday rituals linger—a reminder that in the sacred rhythms of the season, there is a space for reflection, transformation, and the eternal hope for a year of sweetness, blessing, and renewal.

Shofar Horn Blowing: A Call to the Soul

At the heart of Rosh Hashanah, the Jewish New Year, reverberates a primal and soul-stirring sound—the resonant blast of the shofar. As communities gather in synagogues and homes, the haunting notes of this ceremonial ram's horn echo through the air, symbolizing not only the arrival of a new year but also a profound call to spiritual awakening, reflection, and repentance. In this exploration of the Shofar Horn Blowing, we delve into the significance, history, and spiritual resonance of this ancient practice that has endured for millennia.

The Origins and Symbolism of the Shofar:

The shofar holds a unique place in Jewish tradition, tracing its roots back to the biblical narratives of the Hebrew Scriptures. The word "shofar" itself is derived from the Hebrew root Shin-Pe-Resh, which signifies beauty or excellence. This choice of language already imbues the horn with a sense of sacredness, suggesting that the shofar is not just an instrument; it is an expression of divine beauty and excellence.

The shofar is most commonly made from the horn of a ram, although the horns of other kosher animals, such as goats, can also be used. The choice of the ram's horn carries its own symbolism, evoking the biblical narrative of the

Binding of Isaac, where a ram was provided as a substitute for Isaac. The shofar thus becomes a symbolic reminder of sacrifice, divine intervention, and the covenant between God and the Jewish people.

The Commandment to Hear the Shofar:

The practice of blowing the shofar is deeply rooted in the commandments outlined in the Torah. In the Book of Leviticus (23:24-25), Rosh Hashanah is referred to as "Zikhron Teruah," meaning a remembrance of the shofar blast. The Torah instructs that on this day, a holy convocation is to be proclaimed, and the shofar is to be sounded. This biblical mandate underscores the centrality of the shofar in the observance of Rosh Hashanah.

The sounding of the shofar is not merely a cultural or symbolic gesture; it is a divine commandment that transcends time and generations. The echoes of the shofar connect contemporary worshippers with the ancient Israelites who stood before Mount Sinai, underscoring the enduring nature of this sacred practice.

The Structure of Shofar Blowing: Tekiah, Shevarim, Teruah, Tekiah Gedolah:

The shofar blowing during Rosh Hashanah follows a specific and structured sequence, consisting of four primary sounds: Tekiah, Shevarim, Teruah, and Tekiah Gedolah.

1. Tekiah (תְּקִיעָה): The first and longest note, representing a solid, unbroken sound. It serves as a call to attention, a proclamation of divine kingship, and an invitation to introspection.

2. Shevarim (שְׁבָרִים): A set of three broken, staccato notes. This sound is likened to the sobbing of a contrite heart and serves as a reminder of human frailty and the need for repentance.

3. Teruah (תְּרוּעָה): A series of nine rapid, short blasts, resembling an alarm or a wailing cry. Teruah is associated with the theme of awakening, a call to action, and a recognition of the urgency of repentance.

4. Tekiah Gedolah (תְּקִיעָה גְּדוֹלָה): The final, long blast that concludes the sequence. Tekiah Gedolah is an extended note, often held for an extended period, representing the culmination of the shofar blowing and the hope for a year filled with blessings.

This structured sequence is repeated multiple times during the Rosh Hashanah services, creating a rhythmic and symbolic journey that resonates with worshippers on both an emotional and spiritual level.

The Mystical Significance of Shofar Sounds:

Beyond the literal interpretation of the shofar sounds, Jewish mysticism, particularly in the Kabbalistic tradition, explores deeper meanings associated with each sound. The teachings of Kabbalah delve into the mystical dimensions of the Hebrew letters and their numerical values, connecting the shofar sounds with the divine attributes and the cosmic order.

In Kabbalistic interpretation, the Tekiah is associated with the divine attribute of Chesed, representing kindness and benevolence. Shevarim corresponds to Gevurah, symbolizing severity and judgment. Teruah is linked to the divine emanation of Tiferet, representing beauty and balance. The final Tekiah Gedolah is connected with Keter, the crown, representing the highest and most transcendent divine aspect.

Through this lens, the shofar becomes a conduit for accessing and harmonizing with the divine energies, providing a mystical pathway for worshippers to connect with the celestial realms during the High Holidays.

The Spiritual Journey of Shofar Blowing:

The shofar blowing on Rosh Hashanah is more than a ritual; it is a spiritual journey that unfolds in the hearts and souls of those who listen. The intentional sequence of sounds creates a narrative that mirrors the human experience—the steady call to attention, the brokenness of the human condition, the urgent cry for awakening, and the hopeful culmination of renewal and blessing.

As the shofar sounds resonate through the sanctuary or the home, worshippers are invited to embark on a personal odyssey of reflection and repentance. The shofar becomes a sacred vessel, carrying the collective prayers, aspirations, and confessions of the community, lifting them towards the divine and facilitating a profound encounter between the human and the transcendent.

The Shofar in Historical Context:

The shofar has witnessed and participated in the unfolding of Jewish history, standing as a witness to triumphs, trials, and tribulations. Throughout the centuries, in times of joy and sorrow, the shofar has sounded its call, echoing the resilience and enduring spirit of the Jewish people.

During the Second Temple period, the shofar played a prominent role in the liturgical practices of the Holy Temple in Jerusalem. The sounding of the shofar marked the New Year and was also associated with other momentous occasions, such as the coronation of kings and the announcement of the Jubilee year.

However, with the destruction of the Second Temple in 70 CE, the use of the shofar in the Temple rituals ceased.

Despite this loss, the shofar continued to be a symbol of resilience and hope for the Jewish people in the face of adversity. Its use during Rosh Hashanah became even more pronounced, carrying the weight of historical continuity and the unbroken connection between past, present, and future.

Geographic and Cultural Variations in Shofar Blowing:

The practice of shofar blowing is not uniform across all Jewish communities; rather, it exhibits geographic and cultural variations that add to the richness of the tradition. Different Jewish communities may have distinct customs regarding the length, style, and specific tunes associated with shofar blowing.

For example, Sephardic and Ashkenazi traditions may have variations in the melodies used during the shofar service, reflecting the diverse cultural influences that have shaped these communities over centuries. Additionally, the Yemenite Jewish community has its own unique style of shofar blowing, incorporating distinct tunes and cadences that reflect their cultural heritage.

In some communities, particularly those in the Middle East, the shofar is often embellished with intricate silver or gold decorations, adding an extra layer of aesthetic beauty to this sacred instrument. These cultural nuances demonstrate the adaptability and diversity of the shofar tradition, allowing it to resonate with the unique cultural contexts of different Jewish communities around the world.

The Shofar in Modern Context:

In the contemporary era, the shofar continues to hold its revered place in the observance of Rosh Hashanah, and its sound remains a potent and evocative symbol for Jews worldwide. The shofar's call transcends physical boundaries, reaching Jews in diverse settings—from bustling urban centers to remote villages—and uniting them in a shared spiritual experience.

Technological advancements have also played a role in extending the reach of the shofar's sound. Livestreamed services, virtual gatherings, and online platforms have made it possible for individuals around the world to listen to the shofar even if they cannot be physically present in a synagogue. The shofar's call, once limited to the walls of a sanctuary, can now resonate in the homes of individuals across continents, fostering a sense of unity and connection within the global Jewish community.

Moreover, the shofar has found resonance beyond the Jewish community, becoming a symbol of interfaith dialogue and understanding. Its distinctive sound has been featured in various cultural events, concerts, and collaborative projects, creating bridges of appreciation and respect between diverse communities.

Shofar Blowing and Personal Transformation:

The essence of the shofar blowing extends beyond its historical, cultural, or religious dimensions; it is an invitation to personal transformation. The sounds of the shofar serve as a catalyst for introspection, prompting individuals to examine their deeds, seek forgiveness, and aspire towards spiritual growth.

Each individual's response to the shofar is deeply personal, influenced by their life experiences, struggles, and triumphs. For some, the shofar may evoke a sense of awe and reverence, while for others, it may stir emotions of joy, repentance, or introspection. The shofar's call is a universal language that speaks to the human soul, transcending linguistic and cultural barriers.

Contemporary Innovations in Shofar Blowing:

In recent years, there has been a resurgence of interest in innovative and creative approaches to shofar blowing. Artists, musicians, and cultural enthusiasts have explored new ways to incorporate the shofar's sound into various artistic mediums, blending tradition with contemporary expression.

Experimental compositions, collaborative performances, and multimedia presentations have emerged, showcasing the versatility of the shofar and its ability to adapt to diverse artistic expressions. The shofar's ancient sound, once confined to religious ceremonies, has now become a source of inspiration for creative endeavors that span the boundaries of tradition and modernity.

Conclusion: The Timeless Echoes of the Shofar:

As we conclude our exploration of the Shofar Horn Blowing in the context of Rosh Hashanah, the echoes of this ancient practice linger—a testament to its enduring significance and spiritual resonance. The shofar's call is more than a musical sequence; it is a bridge between the earthly and the divine, a conduit for personal and communal transformation, and a timeless reminder of the sacred cycle of renewal.

In the chapters that follow, we will continue our journey into the depths of Rosh Hashanah's traditions, exploring the rich symbolism, customs, and rituals that define this sacred season. The shofar, with its primal sound, will accompany us, serving as a guide and a companion on the spiritual odyssey that unfolds during the Jewish New Year—a journey marked by introspection, repentance, and the hopeful anticipation of a year filled with blessings and renewal.

Tashlich Casting Off Sins: A Ritual of Renewal by the Water's Edge

As the sun dips below the horizon on Rosh Hashanah, the Jewish New Year, a unique and symbolic ritual unfolds along riverbanks, lakeshores, and coastal edges—Tashlich. This ancient custom, rooted in both spiritual depth and poetic symbolism, invites participants to cast off their sins into the flowing waters, marking a profound act of cleansing, repentance, and spiritual renewal. In this exploration of "Tashlich Casting Off Sins," we delve into the historical origins, symbolic significance, and contemporary expressions of this evocative Rosh Hashanah practice.

Origins and Historical Context:

The term "Tashlich" is derived from the Hebrew word "tashlikh," meaning "cast off" or "throw." The ritual finds its roots in the biblical text of Micah 7:19: "You will cast all their sins into the depths of the sea." This verse served as the inspiration for the Tashlich custom, framing it within the context of divine forgiveness and the symbolic casting away of transgressions.

Historically, Tashlich is believed to have emerged in medieval Europe, gaining popularity among Jewish communities during the 14th and 15th centuries. The ritual served as a tangible and communal expression of repentance, aligning with the spiritual themes of Rosh Hashanah as a time of reflection, self-examination, and the pursuit of forgiveness.

The Symbolism of Water:

Central to the Tashlich ritual is the choice of a body of flowing water, such as a river, stream, or ocean. Water, in its dynamic and transformative nature, becomes a powerful symbol in Jewish tradition, representing both life and purification. The selection of water for Tashlich is not arbitrary; it reflects a deep understanding of the symbolic journey undertaken by participants as they engage in this ancient ritual.

The flowing water serves as a metaphor for the passage of time and the ever-renewing cycle of life. Just as water is in constant motion, participants in Tashlich are invited to let go of their past transgressions, allowing them to be carried away by the current. The act of casting sins into the water becomes a visual and visceral representation of releasing the burdens of the past and embracing the possibility of spiritual rebirth.

The Ritual Practice of Tashlich:

The Tashlich ritual is typically conducted on the afternoon of the first day of Rosh Hashanah, a time when communities gather near bodies of water to partake in this collective act of repentance. The ceremony itself is straightforward yet imbued with profound symbolism.

Participants stand by the water's edge, often reciting specific prayers and passages from the Psalms that emphasize divine forgiveness and the casting away of sins. Traditional Tashlich prayers may include verses such as Micah 7:19, Psalms 118:5-9, and Psalms 33:18-22, each contributing to the spiritual ambiance of the ritual.

As the prayers are recited, individuals may choose to carry breadcrumbs or small pieces of bread, representing their sins, which they then cast into the water. The act of casting off these symbolic burdens is accompanied by personal reflections, confessions, and expressions of remorse. Participants may take a moment to contemplate the specific actions or behaviors they seek to relinquish, allowing the ritual to become a deeply personal and introspective experience.

Metaphorical Aspects of Tashlich:

Beyond the literal casting away of breadcrumbs, Tashlich possesses metaphorical layers that deepen its significance. The act of casting sins into the water becomes a metaphor for the cleansing of the soul, akin to a spiritual purification. The flowing water, in its perpetual motion, mirrors the cyclical nature of life and the opportunities for renewal that come with each passing year.

In the act of Tashlich, individuals confront the tangible representation of their mistakes and transgressions, acknowledging their imperfections and shortcomings. Yet, by releasing these symbolic burdens into the water, participants express their hope for forgiveness and transformation. The ritual becomes a poignant reminder that, just as water can wash away physical impurities, the soul too can undergo a process of purification and renewal.

Variations in Tashlich Practices:

While the core elements of Tashlich remain consistent, variations in the ritual exist among different Jewish communities. Some may choose to recite specific liturgical poems or incorporate additional prayers, adding cultural and regional nuances to the ceremony. The choice of water bodies can also vary, ranging from natural bodies of water to specially constructed ritual pools.

In certain communities, particularly those with environmental concerns, efforts are made to ensure that the materials used in Tashlich are environmentally friendly. Biodegradable items, such as bird-friendly crackers, may be substituted for traditional breadcrumbs, aligning the ritual with contemporary values of ecological responsibility.

The Personal Journey of Tashlich:

As individuals engage in the Tashlich ritual, they embark on a deeply personal and introspective journey. The act of standing by the water's edge, contemplating one's actions, and casting off symbolic representations of sin is a visceral and emotional process. Tashlich provides a tangible outlet for the complex emotions associated with repentance—guilt, remorse, humility, and the earnest desire for forgiveness.

In this moment of reflection, participants may find solace in the rhythmic sounds of the water, the rustling leaves, and the communal recitation of prayers. The Tashlich experience transcends the individual and becomes a shared journey, connecting participants to a broader community engaged in the same pursuit of spiritual renewal.

The Role of Community in Tashlich:

While Tashlich involves a deeply personal reckoning with one's actions, it is inherently a communal experience. The gathering of individuals by the water's edge creates a shared space for reflection and collective introspection. As participants engage in the ritual simultaneously, there is a profound sense of unity and shared purpose.

Communities may choose to conduct Tashlich in diverse settings, from urban parks to natural landscapes, adapting the ritual to their specific environments. The collective act of casting off sins into the water fosters a sense of solidarity, reminding participants that they are not alone in their quest for spiritual growth and forgiveness.

Contemporary Expressions of Tashlich:

In the modern era, Tashlich has found new expressions and adaptations that resonate with the dynamics of contemporary Jewish life. Technological advancements, particularly in the realm of virtual connectivity, have allowed for innovative approaches to the ritual.

Some communities organize virtual Tashlich experiences, where participants join online gatherings to recite prayers, share reflections, and engage in symbolic acts of casting away sins. While physically distant, these virtual gatherings create a sense of interconnectedness, enabling individuals from diverse locations to participate in Tashlich together.

Additionally, the symbolic aspects of Tashlich have inspired artistic interpretations, with individuals and communities creating visual representations of the ritual. Art installations, paintings, and multimedia presentations capture the essence of Tashlich, offering alternative ways to engage with its profound symbolism.

Conclusion: Tashlich and the Eternal Flow of Renewal:

As we conclude our exploration of Tashlich, the ritual of casting off sins by the water's edge, we recognize its timeless significance in the tapestry of Rosh Hashanah traditions. The act of standing by flowing waters, casting away symbolic burdens, and seeking spiritual renewal is a universal journey undertaken by countless individuals across generations.

In the chapters that follow, we will continue our exploration of Rosh Hashanah's rich traditions, delving into the multifaceted layers of symbolism, customs, and practices that define this sacred season. Tashlich, with its poetic beauty and transformative potential, serves as a poignant reminder that, just as the waters flow endlessly, the opportunities for spiritual renewal and forgiveness are equally boundless.

Chapter 4: Diwali

Victory of Light Story: Illuminating the Spiritual Tapestry of Diwali

In the heart of autumn, as the first stars begin to sparkle in the night sky, millions of people around the world come together to celebrate Diwali—the Festival of Lights. At the core of Diwali lies a profound narrative, a timeless tale that echoes through generations and transcends cultural boundaries—the Victory of Light story. In this exploration, we embark on a journey into the narrative tapestry that defines Diwali, unraveling the layers of mythology, symbolism, and spiritual significance that make the Festival of Lights a beacon of joy and illumination.

The Origins of Diwali: A Tapestry of Myths and Legends:

Diwali, also known as Deepavali, finds its roots in ancient Indian mythology, and its celebration is marked by a convergence of diverse narratives and traditions. While there are variations in the way Diwali is celebrated across regions and communities, the Victory of Light story is a central theme that unites the festival's diverse manifestations.

One of the most revered and widely known versions of the Diwali narrative is the story of Lord Rama, as recounted in the epic Ramayana. According to this tale, Rama, the prince of Ayodhya, embarks on a perilous journey to rescue his wife Sita from the demon king Ravana. The narrative unfolds over fourteen years, culminating in Rama's return to Ayodhya, accompanied by his loyal wife and the monkey god Hanuman.

As the people of Ayodhya joyously welcome Rama, they illuminate the city with an abundance of oil lamps, symbolizing the triumph of light over darkness and good over evil. This iconic moment marks the genesis of the Diwali celebration and sets the stage for the Victory of Light story that continues to be central to Diwali observances.

Symbolism in the Victory of Light:

At its essence, the Victory of Light story encapsulates profound symbolism that resonates with the spiritual teachings embedded in Diwali. The triumph of light over darkness symbolizes the victory of knowledge over ignorance, righteousness over injustice, and the eternal resilience of goodness in the face of adversity.

The oil lamps, or diyas, that illuminate the homes and streets during Diwali serve as powerful symbols of inner enlightenment and the dispelling of ignorance. Each flickering flame represents the innate goodness within individuals and the collective pursuit of a luminous and virtuous life.

Moreover, the Victory of Light story underscores the cyclical nature of life—the inevitable triumph of virtue after periods of struggle and darkness. This cyclical theme aligns with the broader concept of dharma, the righteous path that individuals are encouraged to follow, emphasizing the eternal dance of creation, preservation, and dissolution.

Diwali in Different Traditions: Variations in the Victory of Light Narrative:

While the story of Lord Rama forms a central narrative for Diwali celebrations in many parts of India, diverse cultural and regional traditions have also contributed to the festival's rich tapestry. In some regions, Diwali is associated with the goddess Lakshmi, the embodiment of wealth and prosperity.

According to another narrative, Diwali marks the victory of Lord Krishna over the demon Narakasura, symbolizing the triumph of good over evil. In Sikh tradition, Diwali is observed as Bandi Chhor Divas, commemorating the release of Guru Hargobind Ji from imprisonment.

These variations in the Victory of Light narrative highlight the cultural diversity within the Diwali celebration, demonstrating how the festival has evolved and adapted to the unique histories and beliefs of different communities.

The Story of Lord Rama: An Epic Journey of Virtue and Sacrifice:

The Victory of Light story, as exemplified by the narrative of Lord Rama, unfolds as an epic journey characterized by virtue, sacrifice, and the unwavering pursuit of dharma. Lord Rama, the seventh avatar of Lord Vishnu, embodies the ideals of righteousness, honor, and duty.

The narrative commences with the exile of Rama, his wife Sita, and his loyal brother Lakshmana, from the kingdom of Ayodhya. The demon king Ravana, driven by arrogance and greed, kidnaps Sita, leading to a cosmic battle between the forces of good and evil.

Rama's quest to rescue Sita is not merely a physical journey but a spiritual odyssey—a journey of self-discovery, resilience, and adherence to dharma. Along the way, Rama forms alliances with divine beings, including Hanuman and the monkey army, and faces numerous trials that test his character and commitment to righteousness.

The ultimate culmination of the narrative is Rama's triumphant return to Ayodhya, where the people joyously celebrate his victory by illuminating the city with countless lamps. This moment marks the restoration of dharma and the establishment of a just and righteous rule.

Diwali Preparations: Illuminating Homes and Hearts:

As Diwali approaches, households undergo a transformation, both in terms of physical decorations and spiritual preparations. The Victory of Light story serves as a catalyst for these festive preparations, inspiring individuals to create an atmosphere of warmth, joy, and spiritual reflection.

Homes are adorned with vibrant decorations, rangoli (colorful patterns made on the floor), and strings of twinkling lights. The illumination is not merely an external display but a reflection of the inner radiance that Diwali seeks to awaken within individuals. Cleaning and decorating homes are symbolic acts that signify the removal of physical and spiritual impurities, preparing the space for the arrival of goodness and light.

Diwali sweets and savories, known as mithai, become an integral part of the preparations, symbolizing the sweetness of life and the sharing of joy with loved ones. Gifts are exchanged, and families come together to engage in prayers, rituals, and communal celebrations.

The Significance of Diwali Lamps: Diyas and Beyond:

Central to the Victory of Light narrative is the act of illuminating the darkness with lamps, a practice that has evolved into a central Diwali ritual. Diyas, small oil lamps made of clay, hold a special place in Diwali celebrations, symbolizing the individual's ability to dispel darkness with the light of knowledge and virtue.

As the sun sets on Diwali, homes and public spaces come alive with the warm glow of diyas, creating a mesmerizing tapestry of light. The act of lighting diyas is not a mere tradition but a spiritual offering, a gesture of gratitude, and a reaffirmation of the commitment to goodness and righteousness.

In addition to diyas, decorative lights, lanterns, and electric illuminations have become integral to Diwali decorations in contemporary times. These modern expressions of illumination, while diverging from traditional oil lamps, capture the essence of the Victory of Light story, emphasizing the transformative power of light in dispelling darkness.

Community Celebrations: Diwali as a Time of Togetherness:

Diwali is not just a festival celebrated within the confines of individual homes; it is a communal celebration that fosters a sense of togetherness and shared joy. Community gatherings, cultural events, and public celebrations mark the festive season, bringing people from diverse backgrounds together to revel in the Victory of Light.

In India, Diwali is often accompanied by grand processions, cultural performances, and firework displays that light up the night sky. The communal spirit of Diwali extends beyond geographical boundaries, with Indian communities around the world coming together to celebrate their cultural heritage and the universal message of Diwali.

The Universal Message of Diwali:

Beyond its cultural and religious origins, the Victory of Light story in Diwali conveys a universal message that resonates with people of various faiths and backgrounds. The narrative transcends its specific mythological context to become a timeless parable of hope, resilience, and the enduring capacity of goodness to triumph over darkness.

The symbolic act of lighting lamps during Diwali becomes a universal metaphor for the human journey—a journey marked by challenges, moments of darkness, and the perpetual quest for inner illumination. Diwali invites individuals of all walks of life to reflect on their own paths, to seek the light within, and to share that light with others.

Contemporary Relevance: Diwali in the Modern World:

In the contemporary world, Diwali has taken on new dimensions, adapting to the realities of modern life while retaining its timeless essence. The Victory of Light story continues to inspire individuals to seek higher values, uphold righteousness, and contribute to the well-being of society.

The advent of technology has introduced new ways of celebrating Diwali, with virtual greetings, online celebrations, and social media playing a role in connecting individuals across the globe. In some communities, efforts are made to celebrate an eco-friendly Diwali by minimizing the use of firecrackers and adopting sustainable practices.

Moreover, Diwali's message of inclusivity and the victory of good over evil has found resonance in interfaith dialogue and cultural exchange. Diwali celebrations have become opportunities for people of diverse backgrounds to come together, share in the joy of the festival, and appreciate the universal values it embodies.

Conclusion: Diwali's Ever-Glowing Luminosity:

As we conclude our exploration of the Victory of Light story within the context of Diwali, the Festival of Lights, the ever-glowing luminosity of this celebration lingers—a testament to its enduring significance and universal appeal. The narrative of Diwali, with its layers of mythology, symbolism, and spiritual wisdom, transcends time and space, inviting individuals to immerse themselves in the timeless journey from darkness to light.

In the chapters that follow, we will continue our exploration of Diwali's multifaceted traditions, customs, and rituals, uncovering the diverse ways in which people around the world come together to celebrate the triumph of light, goodness, and the eternal resonance of the Victory of Light story.

Clay Lamp Lighting: Illuminating the Sacred Path of Diwali

In the radiant tapestry of Diwali, the lighting of clay lamps, or diyas, stands as a symbol of profound significance. As the Festival of Lights unfolds, homes, streets, and public spaces come alive with the warm, flickering glow of these humble yet potent symbols. In this exploration of "Clay Lamp Lighting," we delve into the rich tradition of illuminating the darkness with diyas, uncovering the cultural, spiritual, and symbolic dimensions that make this practice an integral part of Diwali celebrations.

The Humble Diya: A Symbol of Illumination and Hope:

At the heart of Diwali celebrations, the diya embodies the essence of illumination, both literal and metaphorical. Crafted from clay or terracotta, the diya is a small, cup-shaped lamp designed to hold oil or ghee (clarified butter) and a cotton wick. Despite its simplicity, the diya carries profound symbolism, symbolizing the triumph of light over darkness, knowledge over ignorance, and the eternal resilience of goodness.

The choice of clay as the material for diyas holds cultural and spiritual significance. Clay is considered pure and natural, reflecting the connection between humanity and the earth. The act of lighting a diya becomes a ritualistic offering, a gesture that bridges the material and spiritual realms, reminding individuals of their interconnectedness with nature and the cosmos.

Diwali's Illuminating Symbolism:

The practice of lighting diyas during Diwali is deeply rooted in the festival's mythology, particularly the Victory of Light story associated with Lord Rama. According to the Ramayana, when Lord Rama, accompanied by his wife Sita and brother Lakshmana, returns to the kingdom of Ayodhya after defeating the demon king Ravana, the people celebrate his homecoming by illuminating the entire city with lamps.

This iconic moment signifies the dispelling of darkness—both physical and metaphorical—and the establishment of righteousness. The act of lighting lamps is seen as a gesture of welcome, a symbolic way for individuals to participate in the joyous celebration of Rama's victory and the triumph of good over evil.

Beyond the Ramayana, the lighting of lamps is also associated with the goddess Lakshmi, who is worshipped during Diwali for her blessings of wealth, prosperity, and good fortune. It is believed that the radiant glow of lamps attracts the goddess, inviting her benevolence into homes and communities.

The Rituals of Diwali Lamp Lighting: A Symphony of Light:

Diwali preparations often commence with a thorough cleaning and decorating of homes, creating a welcoming space for the divine and symbolizing the removal of impurities—both physical and spiritual. As the auspicious day of Diwali arrives, families gather to partake in the ritual of lighting diyas, marking the commencement of the Festival of Lights.

The timing of diya lighting is crucial and is often aligned with the auspicious period known as the "muhurat." Families choose a specific time, usually during the evening, to light the lamps, signifying the transition from daylight to darkness. The act of lighting diyas is accompanied by prayers, hymns, and the recitation of religious verses that invoke divine blessings and express gratitude for the triumph of light.

As the diyas are kindled, their warm glow fills homes with a celestial radiance, creating a serene and uplifting atmosphere. The collective illumination of countless diyas in neighborhoods and communities transforms the darkness of the night into a canvas of shimmering light, symbolizing the shared commitment to goodness and righteousness.

Diwali Diyas: A Symbol of Individual and Collective Enlightenment:

The lighting of diyas during Diwali is not merely a communal practice; it is also a deeply personal and introspective ritual. Each individual diya becomes a symbol of the inner light within, representing the divine spark that resides in every soul. As individuals light their diyas, they are encouraged to contemplate their own journey toward enlightenment, self-discovery, and spiritual awakening.

The flame of the diya is a metaphor for the eternal light of consciousness, a reminder that, even in moments of darkness and uncertainty, the inner light remains unwavering. The act of kindling a diya becomes a personal vow—an affirmation of one's commitment to uphold values, pursue righteousness, and contribute to the betterment of the world.

Moreover, the collective lighting of diyas emphasizes the power of unity and shared purpose. Communities, regardless of differences, come together in a harmonious symphony of light, symbolizing the potential for collective enlightenment and the ability to dispel the shadows of division and discord.

The Spiritual Significance of Diya Light:

In the spiritual context, the diya light holds profound symbolism. The flame represents the atman, the inner self or soul, and its connection to the universal divine. Lighting a diya is not just an external act; it becomes a sacred gesture that awakens the spiritual consciousness within, fostering a sense of devotion, humility, and interconnectedness.

The flickering flame of the diya is a reminder of the impermanence of material existence and the eternal nature of the soul. In the Upanishads, ancient Indian philosophical texts, the analogy of a lamp illuminating a room is often used to convey the illumination of knowledge that dispels the darkness of ignorance.

The act of lighting diyas during Diwali becomes a form of meditation, a moment of quiet reflection in which individuals turn their attention inward, seeking the divine light that resides in the depths of their being. This spiritual dimension adds layers of meaning to the physical act of diya lighting, transforming it into a sacred ritual that transcends the boundaries of time and space.

Artistic Expressions: Diya Designs and Craftsmanship:

The artistic craftsmanship of diyas adds an aesthetic dimension to Diwali celebrations, with artisans showcasing their skill and creativity in the design and decoration of these humble lamps. Diyas come in various shapes, sizes, and colors, reflecting the regional diversity of India and the individual preferences of households.

Traditional diya designs often feature intricate patterns, floral motifs, and auspicious symbols. The use of vibrant colors and natural dyes adds to the visual appeal, creating a visually stunning array of lamps. In contemporary times, artisans also experiment with modern and innovative designs, incorporating elements of fusion that blend tradition with contemporary aesthetics.

Some communities engage in diya painting competitions, where individuals, especially children, showcase their artistic talents by decorating diyas in imaginative ways. These artistic expressions not only add beauty to Diwali decorations but also provide a platform for creativity and cultural expression.

Environmental Consciousness: Sustainable Diya Practices:

In recent years, there has been a growing awareness of the environmental impact of certain Diwali practices, including the materials used in the production of diyas. Traditional diyas, crafted from clay, are biodegradable and eco-friendly. However, the popularity of mass-produced, non-biodegradable diyas made from plaster of Paris (PoP) has raised environmental concerns.

As a response to this, there has been a renewed emphasis on returning to traditional clay diyas and adopting sustainable practices. Eco-friendly diya campaigns encourage individuals to choose clay diyas over PoP alternatives, promoting a consciousness of environmental responsibility during Diwali celebrations.

Additionally, some communities engage in the creation of seed bombs, embedding seeds within clay diyas. After Diwali, these seed bombs can be planted, contributing to the growth of plants and flowers. This innovative approach aligns with the ethos of Diwali, emphasizing the cyclical nature of life and the importance of sustainability.

Diwali Diyas in a Global Context:

While Diwali has its roots in Indian culture and religion, the practice of lighting diyas has transcended geographical boundaries, finding resonance in diverse global contexts. As Indian diaspora communities have spread around the world, Diwali celebrations have become multicultural events, embraced by people of various backgrounds.

In cities across the globe, from London to New York, the iconic imagery of illuminated diyas has become synonymous with the Festival of Lights. Landmarks are often adorned with decorative lights, creating a visual spectacle that symbolizes the universal themes of Diwali—light, hope, and the triumph of good over evil.

In multicultural societies, Diwali has become an occasion for interfaith dialogue, cultural exchange, and community building. The practice of lighting diyas has found common ground with the universal human yearning for light in times of darkness, making Diwali a celebration that transcends cultural and religious boundaries.

Conclusion: The Luminous Legacy of Diwali Diyas:

As we conclude our exploration of "Clay Lamp Lighting" within the context of Diwali, the luminous legacy of diyas continues to shine brightly. From the humble clay lamps of ancient India to the vibrant, artistic expressions of contemporary celebrations, the act of lighting diyas has remained an enduring symbol of illumination, hope, and spiritual awakening.

In the chapters that follow, we will further unravel the intricate traditions, customs, and rituals that define Diwali, exploring the multifaceted layers of this globally celebrated Festival of Lights. The diya, with its timeless radiance, invites us to contemplate the ever-present light within and the collective journey from darkness to illumination.

Feasts and Fireworks: A Banquet of Joy and Spectacle

In the luminous celebration of Diwali, the festivities extend beyond the glow of clay lamps and into the realm of feasts and fireworks. As families come together, homes are adorned, and the night sky is painted with dazzling bursts of light, Diwali transforms into a banquet of joy and spectacle. In this exploration of "Feasts and Fireworks," we unravel the culinary delights and pyrotechnic displays that add vibrant dimensions to the Festival of Lights, embodying the spirit of celebration, abundance, and communal joy.

Feasts of Diwali: A Culinary Extravaganza:

At the heart of Diwali celebrations lies the tradition of sharing and indulging in delectable feasts that reflect the richness of Indian culinary heritage. The feasting aspect of Diwali is not just a gastronomic experience; it is a cultural expression that brings families, friends, and communities together in a spirit of joyous abundance.

The Diwali menu is a tapestry of flavors, textures, and aromas, showcasing a diverse array of dishes that vary across regions and communities. Traditional sweets, known as mithai, take center stage, with classics such as gulab jamun, jalebi, and barfi gracing the tables. These sweets are not just desserts; they are expressions of love, hospitality, and the sweetness of life.

Savory delights also play a crucial role in Diwali feasts, with an array of snacks, appetizers, and main courses that cater to diverse tastes. Samosas, pakoras, chaats, and a variety of curries contribute to the culinary opulence of Diwali, offering a symphony of flavors that tantalize the taste buds.

The Significance of Diwali Sweets:

Mithai, or sweets, hold a special place in Diwali celebrations, symbolizing the sweetness of life, the sharing of joy, and the auspiciousness of the occasion. The preparation of Diwali sweets often begins weeks in advance, with families and communities engaging in the art of confectionery to create homemade delicacies.

Each type of sweet carries its own cultural and regional significance. For example, the round shape of laddoos symbolizes unity and completeness, while the diamond shape of barfi represents wealth and prosperity. The act of exchanging sweets during Diwali is not just a gesture of hospitality; it is a way of expressing good wishes and positive energy.

Diwali Savories: A Culinary Symphony:

In addition to sweets, Diwali feasts feature an array of savory delights that cater to a spectrum of tastes. Samosas, with their crispy pastry and spiced potato filling, are a ubiquitous presence, offering a delightful combination of textures and flavors. Pakoras, deep-fried fritters made with chickpea flour, showcase the versatility of Indian spices and provide a perfect accompaniment to the festive atmosphere.

Chaats, a category of savory street food, also make an appearance on Diwali menus, adding a burst of tangy and spicy flavors. Pani puri, bhel puri, and sev puri are among the popular chaat varieties that capture the essence of Indian street cuisine, creating a lively and interactive dining experience.

Main courses during Diwali often feature an assortment of vegetarian and non-vegetarian dishes that showcase the culinary diversity of India. From rich and creamy paneer dishes to aromatic biryanis and succulent kebabs, the Diwali feast becomes a culinary journey that celebrates the myriad flavors of the subcontinent.

Diwali and Regional Cuisine:

One of the fascinating aspects of Diwali feasts is the regional diversity in culinary traditions that manifests in different parts of India. Each region brings its own unique flavors, ingredients, and cooking techniques to the Diwali table, contributing to the richness and variety of the festive spread.

In North India, for example, the emphasis may be on rich and indulgent dishes such as paneer tikka, butter chicken, and assorted kebabs. The use of cream, ghee, and aromatic spices characterizes the cuisine of this region, creating a sumptuous dining experience.

In South India, Diwali feasts may showcase a variety of rice-based dishes such as biryanis, pulavs, and tamarind rice. The inclusion of coconut, curry leaves, and a medley of spices adds a distinct southern flair to the celebration.

In the western state of Gujarat, Diwali is celebrated with an emphasis on vegetarian dishes. Dhokla, khandvi, and undhiyu are among the traditional Gujarati delicacies that find a place on the Diwali menu, offering a harmonious blend of sweet, savory, and spicy flavors.

In the eastern state of West Bengal, the celebration may feature sweet delicacies such as sandesh, rasgulla, and mishti doi, reflecting the region's penchant for desserts made with chhena (cottage cheese).

The Ritual of Sharing: Community and Generosity:

Central to the Diwali feast is the spirit of sharing and generosity. Families often prepare an abundance of food not only for their own enjoyment but also to share with neighbors, friends, and those less fortunate. The act of exchanging plates of sweets and savories is a common practice, fostering a sense of community and interconnectedness.

In some communities, it is customary to prepare extra portions of Diwali dishes and distribute them to neighbors and friends. This act of sharing goes beyond the immediate circle of family and friends, extending the joy of Diwali to the broader community.

Additionally, many families take the opportunity of Diwali to engage in acts of charity, donating food and essentials to those in need. The act of giving during Diwali becomes a way of spreading the spirit of abundance and compassion, aligning with the festival's underlying themes of prosperity and goodwill.

Diwali and Modern Culinary Trends:

In contemporary times, the culinary landscape of Diwali has seen a fusion of traditional recipes with modern culinary trends. While classic recipes continue to hold sway, some families experiment with innovative dishes, incorporating global flavors and contemporary cooking techniques.

Healthy Diwali recipes have gained popularity, with an emphasis on using fresh, seasonal ingredients and incorporating nutritional elements. Some individuals opt for sugar-free or low-sugar sweets, catering to health-conscious preferences while retaining the festive spirit.

The accessibility of global ingredients and the influence of culinary trends from around the world have also led to the creation of fusion dishes that meld traditional Indian flavors with international cuisines. This blending of culinary traditions reflects the dynamic nature of contemporary Diwali celebrations, where the old and the new coexist in a celebration of diversity.

Fireworks: Illuminating the Night Sky:

As the feasting commences, another dimension of Diwali celebrations unfolds—the spectacular display of fireworks that transforms the night sky into a canvas of light and color. Fireworks, known as "anar" in Hindi, hold a longstanding tradition in Diwali festivities, symbolizing the triumph of light over darkness and the collective joy of the community.

The origins of the Diwali fireworks tradition can be traced back to the belief that the loud sounds and bright lights of fireworks drive away evil spirits. Over time, this practice has evolved into a symbolic celebration of the victory of good over evil, with fireworks becoming an integral part of the Diwali experience.

Fireworks in Diwali Mythology:

The association of fireworks with Diwali finds resonance in various mythological narratives. One such narrative is the story of Lord Krishna's defeat of the demon Narakasura. According to the legend, after the demon's defeat, the people celebrated by lighting oil lamps and bursting fireworks, symbolizing the dispelling of darkness and the triumph of righteousness.

In the Victory of Light story associated with Lord Rama, the lighting of lamps is complemented by the bursting of fireworks, creating a sensory symphony that engages both sight and sound. The joyous explosions of fireworks are seen as a way of expressing exuberance, delight, and the collective celebration of the festival.

The Cultural Significance of Fireworks:

The use of fireworks during Diwali extends beyond their mythological and symbolic connotations to become a cultural and communal expression. Fireworks are a source of joy for people of all ages, creating a festive atmosphere that resonates with the spirit of Diwali.

In addition to their celebratory role, fireworks are also believed to have a spiritual significance. The loud noises produced by fireworks are thought to ward off negative energies and purify the atmosphere, creating a sense of renewal and freshness.

Varieties of Diwali Fireworks: A Kaleidoscope of Light:

Diwali fireworks come in a dazzling array of types and designs, ranging from simple sparklers to elaborate aerial displays. Some of the commonly used fireworks during Diwali include:

1. Sparklers: Handheld fireworks that emit colorful sparks when lit, creating a visual spectacle reminiscent of stars.

2. Fountains: Ground-based fireworks that produce a cascade of sparks, resembling a fountain. These are often used to create decorative patterns.

3. Crackers: Loud fireworks that explode with a bang, adding an auditory element to the visual display. Crackers come in various sizes and intensities.

4. Aerial Shells: Larger fireworks that are launched into the sky and explode, creating a burst of colors and patterns. Aerial shells are a highlight of professional firework displays.

5. Roman Candles: Tube-shaped fireworks that shoot out colored stars and other effects when ignited.

6. Chakras (Spinning Wheels): Fireworks that spin rapidly on the ground, emitting sparks in all directions.

7. Flowerpots: Fireworks that, when ignited, produce a burst of light and color that resembles a blooming flower.

The diversity of Diwali fireworks allows individuals and communities to tailor their celebrations to their preferences, creating a kaleidoscope of light and sound that mirrors the vibrancy of the festival.

Environmental Considerations: Sustainable Celebrations:

While fireworks are an integral part of Diwali celebrations, there has been a growing awareness of their environmental impact. The use of certain chemicals and materials in fireworks can contribute to air and noise pollution, raising concerns about their ecological footprint.

In response to these concerns, some communities have taken steps to promote eco-friendly alternatives or limit the use of fireworks. Sustainable celebrations may involve the use of low-emission fireworks, community-based displays instead of individual celebrations, or a shift toward cultural and artistic events that reduce the reliance on pyrotechnics.

Community Displays and Cultural Celebrations:

In many places, Diwali fireworks are not limited to individual households. Cities and communities often organize public displays that bring people together for a shared experience of joy and wonder. These community displays, often set against iconic landmarks, contribute to a sense of unity and collective celebration.

Additionally, cultural celebrations and events are organized in various parts of the world to mark Diwali. These events may include performances, art installations, and culinary showcases that highlight the richness of Indian culture and the universal themes of Diwali.

Conclusion: The Feast of Light and Sound:

As we conclude our exploration of "Feasts and Fireworks" within the context of Diwali, the vibrant tapestry of this festival comes alive in the feasts that tantalize the taste buds and the fireworks that illuminate the night sky. The culinary delights and pyrotechnic displays of Diwali embody the spirit of celebration, abundance, and shared joy, inviting individuals and communities to partake in a banquet of light and sound.

In the chapters that follow, we will continue our journey through the multifaceted traditions, customs, and rituals that define Diwali, uncovering the diverse ways in which people around the world come together to celebrate the triumph of light, goodness, and the enduring spirit of the Festival of Lights.

Prayer Rituals: Illuminating the Spiritual Essence of Diwali

Amidst the feasts and fireworks that characterize Diwali, the Festival of Lights also encompasses a profound spiritual dimension manifested through prayer rituals. Rooted in ancient traditions and mythology, these rituals serve as a spiritual anchor, connecting individuals to the deeper meanings of Diwali. In this exploration of "Prayer Rituals," we delve into the sacred practices that illuminate the spiritual essence of Diwali, fostering introspection, devotion, and a sense of divine connection.

Diwali: A Time for Spiritual Reflection:

As Diwali dawns, families and communities embark on a journey of spiritual reflection, turning their attention inward and seeking a connection with the divine. The festival's spiritual significance is encapsulated in the belief that the inner light of the soul, akin to the flickering flame of a diya, can dispel the darkness of ignorance and usher in a renewed sense of purpose and clarity.

The spiritual underpinnings of Diwali are embedded in the Victory of Light stories associated with Lord Rama, Lord Krishna, and the goddess Lakshmi. These narratives emphasize the triumph of righteousness, the defeat of inner and outer demons, and the restoration of balance in the cosmos. Diwali becomes a sacred moment to reflect on these timeless teachings and apply them to one's own journey of self-discovery and spiritual growth.

Diwali Prayer Spaces: Sanctuaries of Devotion:

Central to Diwali prayer rituals is the creation of sacred spaces within homes, where families gather to offer prayers, express gratitude, and seek divine blessings. The prayer room or altar, often adorned with vibrant fabrics, flowers, and images of deities, becomes a sanctum of devotion—a place where the sacred and the mundane converge.

The placement of deities such as Lord Rama, Sita, Lakshmana, Lord Krishna, and the goddess Lakshmi holds symbolic significance. These divine beings are revered as embodiments of virtue, wisdom, and prosperity. The act of adorning their images with flowers, garlands, and sacred symbols serves as a gesture of reverence and a means of inviting their divine presence into the home.

Diwali Puja: Invoking Divine Blessings:

The Diwali prayer ritual, known as puja, is a central aspect of the festival's spiritual observances. Families engage in elaborate preparations to conduct the puja, involving the meticulous arrangement of offerings, the lighting of lamps, and the recitation of sacred verses and hymns.

The puja typically begins with the ritualistic cleansing of the home, symbolizing the removal of impurities and the creation of a sacred space for the divine. The act of sprinkling holy water and drawing rangoli designs at the threshold of the home signifies the welcoming of positive energies and divine blessings.

Central to the Diwali puja is the invocation of Lord Ganesha, the remover of obstacles, and Goddess Lakshmi, the bestower of wealth and prosperity. Lord Ganesha is worshipped at the outset of the puja to seek his blessings for the successful completion of the ritual, while Goddess Lakshmi is invoked to shower her divine grace and blessings on the household.

The Act of Aarti: Devotional Hymns and Light Offerings:

A pivotal moment in the Diwali puja is the performance of aarti, a devotional ritual involving the waving of lighted lamps before the deities. Aarti is accompanied by the singing of hymns and devotional songs that express love, gratitude, and surrender to the divine.

As the flame of the aarti lamp dances in the air, its warm glow symbolizes the inner light of the soul. The rhythmic waving of the lamp is not merely a symbolic gesture; it is a profound act of devotion that seeks to connect with the divine presence and express reverence.

The aarti ritual is often conducted with multiple lamps, creating a mesmerizing display of light and sound. Devotees participate in the collective rhythm of aarti, fostering a sense of unity and shared spiritual experience. The resonant melodies and the fragrance of incense add sensory dimensions to the ritual, creating a sacred ambiance that transcends the material realm.

Offerings and Prasad: Symbolic Gestures of Devotion:

Central to Diwali puja are offerings made to the deities, ranging from fruits and flowers to sweets and special dishes prepared for the occasion. These offerings, known as prasad, symbolize the devotee's gratitude and willingness to share the bounty of life with the divine.

Sweets, in particular, hold special significance as offerings to Goddess Lakshmi. The act of presenting sweet delicacies is a gesture of seeking her blessings for a life filled with sweetness, prosperity, and abundance. The distribution of prasad to family members and guests further extends the spirit of sharing and communal joy.

Deepavali: The Illumination of Lamps:

The lighting of lamps, or deepas, is a central theme in Diwali, representing the victory of light over darkness. In the context of prayer rituals, the act of kindling lamps takes on a spiritual significance, symbolizing the awakening of inner light and the dispelling of ignorance.

Devotees often light multiple lamps during the puja, creating a luminous tableau that transforms the prayer space into a radiant sanctuary. The glow of the lamps is not merely a visual spectacle; it is a symbolic expression of the divine illumination that guides individuals on their spiritual journey.

The choice of oil or ghee as fuel for the lamps is laden with symbolism. Oil, derived from seeds, represents the potential for growth and transformation. Ghee, or clarified butter, symbolizes purity and the capacity to dispel darkness. As the lamps burn, the fragrance of the oil or ghee becomes an offering that permeates the surroundings with a sense of sanctity.

Diwali Mantras and Chants: Vibrations of the Sacred Word:

Integral to the Diwali prayer rituals are the recitation of mantras and sacred chants, which hold the power to invoke divine energies and create a vibrational resonance in the environment. Mantras, comprising sacred syllables and sounds, are believed to carry the essence of cosmic energy and divine wisdom.

During the puja, devotees chant specific mantras dedicated to the deities being invoked. The rhythmic repetition of these mantras creates a meditative atmosphere, allowing individuals to attune their minds to the divine presence and experience a sense of inner calm.

The Gayatri Mantra, a revered hymn from the Rig Veda, is often recited during Diwali prayers. This ancient mantra is considered a source of spiritual illumination, embodying the divine light that dispels ignorance and leads to wisdom.

Diwali Vrat and Fasting: Purification of Body and Spirit:

In some traditions, Diwali is observed with vrat (fasting) as a means of purifying the body and spirit. Devotees choose to abstain from certain foods and engage in prayer and introspection throughout the day. The fast is broken after the completion of the evening puja, with a special meal that often includes symbolic foods such as fruits, nuts, and sweets.

Fasting during Diwali is seen as a way of cultivating self-discipline, detoxifying the body, and focusing on the spiritual dimensions of the festival. It is also considered an expression of solidarity with those who may have limited access to food, fostering a sense of empathy and compassion.

Community Prayer Services: Shared Spirituality:

While Diwali prayer rituals are often conducted within the confines of homes, community prayer services also play a significant role in the festival. Temples and spiritual centers organize special prayer sessions, pujas, and satsangs (spiritual discourses) that bring people together in a collective expression of devotion.

Community prayer services serve as a platform for shared spirituality, allowing individuals to connect with the divine in the company of like-minded seekers. The resonance of collective prayers, accompanied by the uplifting melodies of bhajans (devotional songs), creates an atmosphere of spiritual communion that transcends individual boundaries.

Diwali and Global Interfaith Dialogue:

In an increasingly interconnected world, Diwali has become an occasion for interfaith dialogue and shared spirituality. In multicultural societies, people from various religious backgrounds come together to appreciate the universal themes of light, goodness, and the triumph of virtue over vice.

Interfaith Diwali celebrations often involve joint prayer services, cultural exchanges, and collaborative community initiatives. These events emphasize the commonality of human values across diverse faith traditions and foster a sense of unity in diversity.

Conclusion: The Radiant Tapestry of Diwali Prayer Rituals:

As we conclude our exploration of "Prayer Rituals" within the context of Diwali, the radiant tapestry of spiritual practices comes to life. The prayer rituals of Diwali serve as a luminous thread that weaves together the diverse traditions, customs, and celebrations associated with the Festival of Lights.

In the chapters that follow, we will continue our journey through the multifaceted dimensions of Diwali, exploring the rich symbolism, customs, and rituals that define this global celebration of light, renewal, and spiritual awakening.

Chapter 5: Songkran
Water Festival Significance: Embracing Renewal and Joy in the Thai New Year

As the scorching sun heralds the arrival of the Thai New Year, the nation transforms into a vibrant canvas of laughter and water. Songkran, the Water Festival, goes beyond mere celebration—it is a profound expression of cultural and spiritual significance. In this exploration of "Water Festival Significance," we delve into the roots of Songkran, unraveling the deep meanings embedded in the ritualistic splashing of water, the cleansing ceremonies, and the communal joy that defines this exuberant festival.

Songkran: A Tapestry of Tradition and Spirituality:

Songkran, derived from the Sanskrit word "Sankranti," marks the traditional Thai New Year and is celebrated with unparalleled fervor and enthusiasm. Falling in April, during the hottest time of the year, Songkran holds cultural, religious, and astrological significance.

Rooted in Theravada Buddhism, the predominant religion in Thailand, Songkran is not merely a festival of water; it is a time of reflection, purification, and the honoring of elders. The water festivities serve as both a symbolic and practical means of washing away the past year's sins, misfortunes, and impurities, paving the way for a fresh start.

Astrological Significance: Transition and Renewal:

The timing of Songkran is closely tied to the sun's entry into the zodiac sign of Aries, marking the vernal equinox. This astrological transition symbolizes the movement of the sun into a new phase, bringing about changes in weather, seasons, and agricultural cycles.

As the sun transitions, Songkran signifies a period of renewal and rejuvenation. The festival aligns with nature's cycles, emphasizing the interconnectedness of human life with the broader cosmic order. This astrological underpinning adds a spiritual depth to the festivities, framing Songkran as a time for personal and collective rebirth.

Water: Symbol of Purification and Blessings:

Water, the central element of Songkran, carries profound symbolism in Thai culture. Beyond its refreshing and cooling properties, water is seen as a purifying force that cleanses the body, mind, and spirit. The act of pouring or splashing water during Songkran is a symbolic gesture of washing away impurities, bad luck, and negativity.

The water used in Songkran rituals is often infused with fragrant herbs, flowers, or medicinal plants, adding therapeutic qualities to the cleansing process. The use of scented water not only refreshes the body but also imparts a sense of auspiciousness and blessing.

The Three Days of Songkran: Traditional Observances:

Songkran is typically observed over three days, each day carrying specific customs and rituals:

1. Day 1 - Maha Songkran Day: This marks the start of the Thai New Year. It is a day for cleaning homes and preparing for the upcoming celebrations. Devotees may visit temples to make merit, offer prayers, and participate in religious ceremonies.

2. Day 2 - Wan Nao Day: This is a transitional day between the old and new years. It is a time for mid-year cleaning, settling debts, and making amends. The focus is on purification, both physically and spiritually.

3. Day 3 - Wan Thaloeng Sok Day: This day is dedicated to preparing for the New Year. People often visit temples, participate in religious ceremonies, and engage in acts of merit. The water festival festivities intensify, reaching their peak on this day.

Rod Nam Dum Hua Ritual: Paying Respects to Elders:

A hallmark of Songkran is the Rod Nam Dum Hua ritual, where younger individuals pay respects to their elders by pouring scented water over their hands. This gesture is a profound act of filial piety, expressing gratitude and seeking blessings from parents and older family members.

The act of pouring water over the hands is not only a physical cleansing but also a symbolic transfer of merit and good wishes. Elders, in turn, may offer words of wisdom, blessings, and guidance for the upcoming year.

The Joyful Splash: Symbolic Playfulness and Unity:

While Songkran carries deep spiritual significance, it is equally renowned for the exuberant water fights that take place in the streets. The joyful splash of water, often accompanied by laughter and music, is a communal expression of shared joy and unity.

The playful water fights transcend age, social status, and background, bringing people from all walks of life together in a collective celebration. This aspect of Songkran reflects the Thai cultural values of harmony, camaraderie, and the ability to find joy in the midst of life's challenges.

Symbolic Themes in Songkran Water Play:

The water play during Songkran is not merely a chaotic and spontaneous event; it carries symbolic themes that align with the festival's deeper meanings:

1. Cleansing and Renewal: The splashing of water symbolizes the cleansing of the old and the embracing of the

new. Participants engage in water fights with a sense of playfulness, shedding the burdens of the past and welcoming the freshness of the present.

2. Blessing and Good Wishes: The act of pouring scented water over others is a way of imparting blessings and good wishes. The water, infused with positive energy, becomes a vehicle for spreading joy, positivity, and auspiciousness.

3. Unity and Social Harmony: The inclusive nature of Songkran water festivities fosters a sense of unity and social harmony. In the midst of the playful chaos, people from different backgrounds come together, breaking down barriers and celebrating their shared humanity.

4. Humility and Equality: In the midst of water fights, societal hierarchies dissolve, and individuals interact on an equal footing. This fosters a sense of humility and camaraderie, reinforcing the belief that, regardless of status or position, all are equal during Songkran.

Songkran in Modern Times: Balancing Tradition and Tourism:

In contemporary times, Songkran has become a global phenomenon, attracting tourists and revelers from around the world. While the essence of the festival remains rooted in tradition and spirituality, the exuberant water fights have taken center stage in many urban areas.

The influx of tourists has prompted a reflection on how to balance the preservation of cultural authenticity with the demands of modern tourism. Efforts are made to educate visitors about the cultural and spiritual significance of Songkran, encouraging respectful participation in the festivities.

Environmental Considerations: Sustainable Celebrations:

As Songkran has gained popularity, there has been a growing awareness of its environmental impact, particularly in terms of water usage. In response to concerns about water scarcity, some communities and organizers have implemented measures to promote responsible water usage during the festival.

Initiatives include the use of water-saving devices, promoting the recycling of water, and organizing eco-friendly events that prioritize sustainability. These efforts align with the cultural values of respect for nature and harmony with the environment.

Conclusion: Songkran's Watery Tapestry of Renewal:

As we conclude our exploration of "Water Festival Significance" within the context of Songkran, the watery tapestry of this vibrant festival comes into focus. Songkran is not merely a water fight; it is a cultural symphony that harmonizes tradition, spirituality, and joyous celebration.

In the chapters that follow, we will continue our journey through the diverse traditions, customs, and rituals that define Songkran, unraveling the rich cultural tapestry that makes the Thai New Year a unique and cherished celebration of renewal, unity, and communal joy.

New Year Blessings: Invoking Prosperity, Harmony, and Good Fortune in Songkran

As the sun ascends to its zenith, ushering in the Thai New Year, the air resonates with laughter, the streets glisten with water, and a chorus of blessings fills the atmosphere. Songkran, the Water Festival, is not only a time for exuberant celebrations but also a moment for invoking profound blessings. In this exploration of "New Year Blessings," we embark on a journey into the heart of Songkran's spiritual dimension, unraveling the traditional rituals, sacred invocations, and symbolic gestures that pave the way for a year of prosperity, harmony, and good fortune.

The Essence of Songkran Blessings:

Blessings lie at the core of Songkran, representing a collective yearning for auspiciousness, abundance, and well-being. The festival's blessings are more than spoken words; they are sacred intentions woven into the fabric of cultural traditions, rituals, and interpersonal exchanges. As water flows freely, so do the blessings, creating a spiritual current that permeates every aspect of Songkran.

Traditional Blessings: Sacred Words of Good Wishes:

The exchange of traditional blessings is a hallmark of Songkran, symbolizing a collective aspiration for a harmonious and prosperous year ahead. These blessings, often conveyed in the Thai language, encapsulate the spirit of the festival and reflect the cultural values of respect, humility, and interconnectedness.

1. "สวัสดีปีใหม่" (Sawasdee Pee Mai): This common greeting translates to "Happy New Year" and sets the tone for positive and joyous interactions during Songkran. It is a simple yet heartfelt expression of good wishes for the new beginning.

2. "สุขสันต์วันใหม่" (Suk San Wan Mai): This phrase conveys "Happy New Day" and is used to wish others happiness and joy in the coming year. It reflects the idea of each new day as an opportunity for renewal and positivity.

3. "ขอให้โชคดี" (Kor Hai Chok Dee): This blessing translates to "Wishing you good luck" and is extended to invoke fortune, success, and favorable circumstances for the recipient.

4. "หนูหวัดดีปีใหม่" (Noo Wad Dee Pee Mai): A playful blessing often used by children, it means "Wishing you well in the New Year." It adds a youthful and lighthearted touch to the exchange of good wishes.

Rod Nam Dum Hua: Blessings through Water Pouring Rituals:

Central to Songkran blessings is the Rod Nam Dum Hua ritual, a ceremonial pouring of scented water over the hands of elders as a gesture of respect and seeking blessings.

This tradition is a profound embodiment of filial piety and the transmission of positive energy from one generation to the next.

1. Elders' Blessings: As younger individuals pour water over the hands of elders, the act is accompanied by the recitation of blessings. Elders, in turn, bestow their heartfelt wishes for health, happiness, and success upon the younger generation.

2. Symbolic Purification: The water used in Rod Nam Dum Hua is not only a medium for blessings but also a symbol of purification. The act of cleansing represents the washing away of the past year's impurities, sins, and misfortunes, making room for a fresh start.

3. Transference of Merit: The pouring of scented water is not merely a physical act; it is a spiritual exchange. Elders transfer their accumulated merit and positive energy to the younger generation, fostering a continuum of well-being and positive karma.

Temple Visits and Blessing Ceremonies:

Songkran is a time when devout Buddhists visit temples to partake in blessing ceremonies, seek guidance from monks, and make merit through acts of generosity. The temple environment becomes a sacred space where individuals connect with the divine, reflect on their spiritual journey, and receive blessings for the coming year.

1. Monastic Blessings: During Songkran, monks play a pivotal role in the bestowing of blessings. Devotees offer alms to monks, listen to sermons on morality and virtue, and receive blessings in return. The monks' prayers are believed to carry immense spiritual power and bring forth positive energies for the community.

2. Watering the Bodhi Tree: The Bodhi tree, symbolizing enlightenment, is often found in temple courtyards. Devotees engage in the ritual of watering the Bodhi tree, expressing gratitude for the Buddha's teachings and seeking blessings for personal and collective well-being.

3. Circumambulation of Temples: Devotees may perform the ritual of walking clockwise around temple grounds, known as circumambulation. This act is accompanied by prayers and meditations, invoking blessings and cultivating a sense of mindfulness and devotion.

The Symbolism of Water Blessings:

Water, in the context of Songkran, is not merely a physical element; it is laden with symbolic significance, carrying layers of meaning that contribute to the blessings bestowed during the festival.

1. Cleansing and Purification: The act of pouring water is a symbolic cleansing, representing the purification of body, mind, and spirit. Water washes away the remnants of the past, creating a space for renewal and a fresh start in the coming year.

2. Flow of Positive Energy: Water, as it flows, symbolizes the unbroken flow of positive energy. Blessings conveyed through water rituals are believed to carry this positive energy, fostering a sense of well-being, harmony, and abundance.

3. Connection with Nature: Songkran's water rituals align with Thailand's agricultural roots. Water is not only a symbol of blessing but also a vital resource for nurturing the earth. The festival's water-related activities pay homage to the interconnectedness between nature, agriculture, and human life.

Traditional Blessings for Specific Occasions:

Songkran encompasses a variety of rituals and blessings tailored for specific occasions and relationships:

1. Family Blessings: Within families, blessings are exchanged with a focus on familial harmony, unity, and prosperity. Elders may offer specific blessings to each family member, tailoring their wishes to individual aspirations and challenges.

2. Friendship Blessings: Friends exchange blessings that emphasize mutual happiness, success, and lifelong camaraderie. The playful atmosphere of Songkran extends to friendships, fostering a sense of shared joy and celebration.

3. Community Blessings: In communal settings, such as neighborhoods or villages, blessings are extended to ensure collective prosperity, security, and well-being. The spirit of unity and cooperation is emphasized, reinforcing the idea that the fortunes of individuals are intertwined with the community.

The Wai: A Gesture of Respect and Blessing:

Integral to the Thai culture of respect is the traditional gesture of the wai—a slight bow with palms pressed together, resembling a prayer position. The wai is not only a sign of respect but also a means of conveying blessings and good wishes.

1. Respect for Elders: The wai is often accompanied by a verbal blessing when performed to show respect to elders. This gesture reflects the cultural emphasis on acknowledging the wisdom and experience of older generations.

2. Reciprocal Blessings: When two individuals wai each other simultaneously, it becomes a mutual exchange of blessings. The act embodies the reciprocity of goodwill and creates a harmonious energy between the participants.

Contemporary Expressions of Songkran Blessings:

In modern times, Songkran has evolved to incorporate contemporary expressions of blessings. Social media platforms, online messages, and digital communication play a role in extending good wishes to a broader audience. Hashtags like #SawasdeePeeMai become virtual avenues for sharing blessings, fostering a sense of connectedness in the digital age.

Conclusion: Songkran's Tapestry of Blessings:

As we conclude our exploration of "New Year Blessings" within the context of Songkran, the tapestry of this vibrant festival unfolds. Songkran's blessings are not just verbal expressions; they are sacred threads that weave through the rituals, traditions, and shared moments of joy, creating a rich and meaningful celebration of renewal, harmony, and prosperity.

In the chapters that follow, we will continue our journey through the diverse traditions, customs, and rituals that define Songkran, unraveling the layers of cultural significance that make the Thai New Year a unique and cherished celebration of blessings and good fortune.

Parades and Parties: A Festive Tapestry of Joy in Songkran

As the Thai New Year dawns, the streets come alive with vibrant processions, pulsating music, and a kaleidoscope of colors. Songkran, the Water Festival, transcends traditional rituals to embrace a spirited celebration through parades and parties. In this exploration of "Parades and Parties," we immerse ourselves in the dynamic festivities that characterize Songkran, unraveling the exuberant parades, lively street parties, and the cultural tapestry that weaves together a joyous celebration of renewal and community.

The Evolution of Songkran Celebrations:

Songkran has evolved over the years from a primarily religious and family-oriented celebration to a nationwide festival that embraces the spirit of communal joy. Parades and parties have become integral components of Songkran, adding a dynamic and inclusive dimension to the festivities.

1. Historical Roots: Songkran's roots can be traced to the ancient practice of sprinkling water on Buddha images and the elderly as a gesture of respect and purification. Over time, the festival transformed into a more public and collective celebration, with parades and parties reflecting the changing dynamics of Thai society.

2. Community Spirit: Parades and parties in Songkran serve as expressions of community spirit. They bring together people from different backgrounds, fostering a sense of unity and shared joy. The celebration transcends individual and familial boundaries, creating a tapestry of cultural diversity within the larger framework of Thai identity.

Songkran Parades: A Colorful Spectacle of Culture and Tradition:

1. Traditional Processions: Songkran parades often feature traditional processions that showcase the rich cultural heritage of Thailand. Elaborately decorated floats, cultural performances, and participants dressed in traditional attire contribute to the visual splendor of the parade.

2. Religious Representations: Many Songkran parades include representations of Buddhist themes and deities. Floats adorned with floral decorations and religious symbols create a sacred ambiance, emphasizing the festival's spiritual underpinnings.

3. Local Art and Crafts: Communities use the parades as platforms to showcase local art, craftsmanship, and traditional skills. Floats may feature intricate floral

arrangements, handmade crafts, and displays that highlight the unique cultural identity of each region.

4. Musical Ensembles: Traditional Thai music and dance troupes often accompany the parades, adding a rhythmic and melodic element to the festivities. The music serves not only as entertainment but also as a cultural expression that connects participants and spectators to Thailand's artistic heritage.

Street Parties: Spirited Celebrations of Unity:

1. Water Fights and Merriment: Street parties during Songkran are synonymous with water fights. Revelers armed with water guns, buckets, and hoses engage in friendly water battles, creating a carnival-like atmosphere. The playful splashing of water serves as a symbol of purification and collective joy.

2. Colorful Powder Smearing: In addition to water, colorful powders are often used during Songkran street parties. Participants smear each other with vibrant powders, creating a spectacle of colors reminiscent of traditional Holi celebrations. The powders symbolize the diversity and vibrancy of life.

3. Live Music and Performances: Street parties feature live music performances, dance shows, and cultural displays that enhance the festive atmosphere. Local and international

artists may take the stage, providing entertainment for the gathered crowds.

4. Food and Street Cuisine: Songkran street parties are a feast for the senses, with an array of street food stalls offering traditional Thai delicacies. The aroma of grilled meats, the sizzle of woks, and the sweet fragrance of desserts create a culinary tapestry that complements the festive mood.

Symbolic Themes in Songkran Parades and Parties:

1. Celebration of Water: The centrality of water in Songkran parades and parties symbolizes the cleansing of the old year and the ushering in of the new. Water fights, water splashing, and the use of colorful powders collectively represent the rejuvenation of body, mind, and spirit.

2. Cultural Harmony: The diversity of cultural expressions in parades reflects Thailand's cultural tapestry. By showcasing traditional art forms, rituals, and crafts, communities celebrate the harmonious coexistence of diverse cultural elements within the broader Thai identity.

3. Community Cohesion: Parades and parties serve as catalysts for community cohesion, bringing people together in a shared celebration. The collective participation in water-related activities fosters a sense of belonging and shared joy, transcending individual differences.

4. Joyful Expression: The lively and spirited nature of Songkran parades and parties reflects the Thai cultural ethos of celebrating life with joy. The festive atmosphere encourages spontaneous expressions of happiness, laughter, and camaraderie.

Regional Variations in Songkran Celebrations:

1. Bangkok: As the capital city, Bangkok's Songkran celebrations are grand and diverse. Parades feature a mix of traditional and contemporary elements, and street parties in popular areas like Khao San Road draw both locals and tourists.

2. Chiang Mai: Chiang Mai is renowned for its elaborate Songkran celebrations, including the famous "moat battles" where participants line the historic city's moat to engage in water fights. Parades in Chiang Mai often highlight the region's unique cultural traditions.

3. Phuket: In Phuket, Songkran festivities blend with the island's beach culture. Beach parties, water events, and cultural parades add a coastal flavor to the celebrations, attracting both locals and international visitors.

4. Sukhothai: The historical city of Sukhothai, considered the birthplace of Songkran, hosts traditional celebrations that harken back to the festival's origins. The

Sukhothai Historical Park becomes a backdrop for cultural processions and rituals.

Preserving Tradition in Contemporary Celebrations:

1. Balancing Modernity and Tradition: The integration of modern elements, such as live music, dance performances, and contemporary art, into Songkran celebrations reflects a dynamic balance between preserving tradition and embracing the evolving cultural landscape.

2. Educating on Cultural Significance: Efforts are made to educate participants and spectators about the cultural significance of Songkran. Information booths, cultural displays, and interactive activities aim to enhance public understanding and appreciation of the festival's roots.

3. Sustainable Practices: In recent years, there has been a growing awareness of the environmental impact of Songkran celebrations, particularly in terms of water usage and waste generation. Some communities are adopting sustainable practices, such as water-saving initiatives and waste reduction measures, to ensure the festival's long-term viability.

Conclusion: The Joyous Tapestry of Songkran Celebrations:

As we conclude our exploration of "Parades and Parties" within the context of Songkran, the joyous tapestry of this vibrant festival comes into focus. Songkran's parades and parties are not mere spectacles; they are dynamic expressions of cultural richness, community spirit, and the collective celebration of life.

In the chapters that follow, we will continue our journey through the diverse traditions, customs, and rituals that define Songkran, unraveling the layers of cultural significance that make the Thai New Year a unique and cherished celebration of joy, unity, and renewal.

Cleansing Rituals: Purification and Renewal in Songkran

As the Thai New Year unfolds, the echoes of laughter mingle with the splashing of water, creating a symphony of purification and renewal. Songkran, the Water Festival, transcends mere merriment to encompass profound cleansing rituals deeply embedded in the cultural fabric of Thailand. In this exploration of "Cleansing Rituals," we immerse ourselves in the symbolic and spiritual dimensions of Songkran, unveiling the diverse rituals that cleanse not only the body but also the soul, marking the beginning of a fresh and auspicious year.

Water as a Symbol of Purification:

At the heart of Songkran's cleansing rituals lies the transformative power of water. More than a physical element, water symbolizes purity, renewal, and the washing away of impurities. The use of water in Songkran rituals reflects a spiritual journey toward a cleansed and refreshed existence.

1. Spiritual Cleansing: Songkran's roots in Theravada Buddhism influence the emphasis on spiritual purification. Water is not just a physical cleanser but a means of purifying the mind and spirit. The act of splashing or pouring water

represents the cleansing of negative thoughts, actions, and past misdeeds.

2. Symbolic Renewal: Water, in its flowing nature, symbolizes the constant cycle of renewal. Songkran coincides with the arrival of spring, aligning with nature's cycles of rebirth. The festival's rituals mirror this natural renewal, inviting individuals to shed the old and welcome the new with open hearts.

3. Community Harmony: The communal aspect of water-related activities fosters a sense of harmony and unity. Engaging in cleansing rituals collectively reinforces the interconnectedness of individuals within the community, emphasizing shared purification and renewal.

The Rod Nam Dum Hua Ceremony: A Touch of Reverence and Blessings:

Central to Songkran's cleansing rituals is the Rod Nam Dum Hua ceremony—a ritualistic pouring of scented water over the hands of elders, monks, and revered figures. This ceremonial act extends beyond the physical to symbolize respect, gratitude, and the seeking of blessings for the year ahead.

1. Filial Piety and Respect: Younger individuals express filial piety by performing the Rod Nam Dum Hua ritual. The act of pouring water over the hands of elders is a

tangible gesture of respect and gratitude, acknowledging their wisdom and experience.

2. Transfer of Blessings: The water used in the ceremony is often infused with fragrant herbs and flowers, imbuing it with symbolic significance. As water is poured, the transfer of blessings takes place, with elders bestowing well-wishes for health, happiness, and prosperity upon the younger generation.

3. Symbolism of Purification: Beyond the exchange of blessings, the pouring of scented water holds deep symbolic meaning. It represents the purification of the body, mind, and spirit, aligning with the festival's overarching theme of cleansing and renewal.

Temple Visits and Merit-Making:

1. Paying Homage to Buddha: Songkran prompts devout Buddhists to visit temples during the festival, engaging in acts of merit-making. This may include offering alms to monks, participating in religious ceremonies, and performing rituals that express devotion to the teachings of Buddha.

2. Watering Bodhi Trees: The Bodhi tree, under which the Buddha is said to have attained enlightenment, holds special significance during Songkran. Devotees engage in the ritual of watering Bodhi trees as a gesture of reverence,

expressing gratitude for the enlightenment that Buddha's teachings bring.

3. Circumambulation of Temple Grounds: Devotees may partake in the ritual of circumambulation—walking clockwise around the temple grounds. This meditative practice, accompanied by prayers and reflections, is a symbolic act of cleansing and renewal, aligning individuals with the spiritual essence of Songkran.

Symbolic Elements in Cleansing Rituals:

1. Herbal Infusions in Water: The water used in cleansing rituals is often infused with herbs and flowers, adding aromatic and therapeutic qualities. The choice of herbs carries symbolic significance, with each plant contributing to the cleansing and purifying intentions of the ritual.

2. White Clothing: Traditional attire during Songkran often includes white clothing. White symbolizes purity and cleanliness, reflecting the aspirational theme of shedding impurities and starting anew. Participants don white garments to embody the essence of spiritual and physical cleansing.

3. Blessed Water: Some communities go beyond simple water fights and incorporate rituals where water is blessed by monks or revered individuals. This blessed water

is considered particularly potent in its ability to cleanse and bring about positive energy.

Regional Variations in Cleansing Rituals:

1. Sukhothai: As the historical city where Songkran is believed to have originated, Sukhothai preserves traditional cleansing rituals. Water is poured over Buddha images, and processions feature symbolic elements that honor the festival's historical roots.

2. Chiang Mai: In Chiang Mai, the "moat battles" see locals and visitors engaging in water fights along the city's ancient moat. This lively tradition is both a form of playful celebration and a symbolic cleansing ritual, as participants immerse themselves in the refreshing waters.

3. Ayutthaya: The ancient city of Ayutthaya showcases a mix of traditional and contemporary cleansing rituals. Temple ceremonies, processions, and water fights contribute to a vibrant celebration that merges the old and the new.

4. Rural Communities: In rural areas, Songkran rituals often involve the cleansing of Buddha images in local temples, followed by community-wide water fights and festivities. These intimate gatherings emphasize the collective nature of purification and renewal.

Environmental Considerations and Sustainable Practices:

1. Water Conservation: In recent years, there has been a growing awareness of water scarcity and environmental impact during Songkran. Some communities have adopted water-saving measures, encouraging participants to use water responsibly and promoting awareness of the importance of conservation.

2. Eco-Friendly Celebrations: Efforts are made to promote eco-friendly practices during Songkran, such as the use of natural dyes in powders and minimizing plastic waste. These initiatives align with the cultural values of respect for nature and the environment.

3. Community Education: Public awareness campaigns aim to educate participants and spectators about the environmental impact of Songkran celebrations. Information booths, signage, and community outreach programs play a role in promoting responsible and sustainable practices.

Conclusion: Songkran's Rituals of Renewal:

As we conclude our exploration of "Cleansing Rituals" within the context of Songkran, the essence of purification and renewal comes into focus. Beyond the joyful water fights and colorful celebrations, Songkran's rituals weave a tapestry of cultural traditions, spirituality, and a collective aspiration for a fresh beginning.

In the chapters that follow, we will continue our journey through the diverse traditions, customs, and rituals that define Songkran, unraveling the layers of cultural significance that make the Thai New Year a unique and cherished celebration of cleansing, renewal, and positive transformation.

Chapter 6: Nowruz

Zoroastrian History: Illuminating the Origins of Nowruz

In the vibrant tapestry of global celebrations, Nowruz stands as a beacon of renewal and hope, a tradition that transcends time and culture. To truly understand the depth and significance of Nowruz, we must delve into its roots, anchored in the rich history of Zoroastrianism. This exploration of "Zoroastrian History" unveils the ancient origins and foundational beliefs that have shaped Nowruz into the profound and enduring festival of new beginnings.

The Dawn of Zoroastrianism:

1. Prophet Zarathustra: The genesis of Zoroastrianism is intertwined with the life and teachings of Prophet Zarathustra (also known as Zoroaster), a visionary figure believed to have lived around the 6th or 7th century BCE. Zarathustra received divine revelations, compiling them into the sacred scripture known as the Avesta.

2. Foundational Teachings: At the core of Zoroastrianism lies the belief in Ahura Mazda, the supreme god representing wisdom and goodness. The cosmic struggle between Ahura Mazda and Angra Mainyu, the destructive force, defines the dualistic nature of Zoroastrian theology.

3. Faravahar Symbol: The Faravahar, an iconic symbol associated with Zoroastrianism, embodies spiritual concepts such as individual responsibility, choice between good and evil, and the eternal nature of the soul. This symbol continues to resonate within Zoroastrian communities and plays a role in Nowruz celebrations.

Zoroastrian Cosmology and Sacred Elements:

1. Elements of Nature: Zoroastrian cosmology revolves around the reverence for natural elements—fire, water, earth, and air. These elements are considered sacred, embodying purity and divine energy. Fire, in particular, holds a central place in Zoroastrian rituals, reflecting the eternal light of Ahura Mazda.

2. Fire Temples: Zoroastrian worship often takes place in fire temples, where the sacred fire is maintained continuously. The fire symbolizes purity and acts as a focal point for spiritual devotion. The reverence for fire finds resonance in Nowruz, where bonfires play a significant role in the festivities.

3. Yazatas and Divine Beings: Zoroastrianism acknowledges the existence of divine beings known as Yazatas, who serve Ahura Mazda. Each Yazata is associated with specific aspects of nature, embodying the divine order that governs the universe.

Zoroastrian Influence on Nowruz:

1. Transition from Darkness to Light: Zoroastrianism's emphasis on the cosmic struggle between light and darkness is mirrored in Nowruz's symbolism. The arrival of spring and the vernal equinox signify the triumph of light over darkness, aligning with Zoroastrian concepts of renewal and the eternal battle between good and evil.

2. Haft Seen and Zoroastrian Symbols: The Haft Seen table, a central element of Nowruz celebrations, features items starting with the Persian letter "S" and holds deep symbolic meanings. Some elements, such as Sabzeh (sprouted wheat or barley), Samanu (sweet pudding), and Senjed (oleaster fruit), have connections to Zoroastrian traditions and agricultural symbolism.

3. Chaharshanbe Suri Fire Jumping: The Chaharshanbe Suri, a prelude to Nowruz, involves jumping over bonfires to cleanse oneself of the past year's impurities. This ritual has echoes of Zoroastrian fire veneration and purification practices.

Zoroastrian Influence on Persian Empire:

1. Cyrus the Great and Religious Tolerance: The Achaemenid Empire, led by Cyrus the Great, was known for its policy of religious tolerance. Cyrus's respect for diverse religious practices, including Zoroastrianism, laid the

foundation for the flourishing of Zoroastrian traditions within the Persian Empire.

2. Cultural Synthesis: The fusion of Zoroastrian beliefs with various cultural elements during the Persian Empire contributed to the rich tapestry of Nowruz. Elements such as the solar calendar, which aligns with Zoroastrian cosmology, became integral to the festival's observance.

Challenges and Resilience:

1. Persecution and Decline: Zoroastrianism faced challenges, particularly during the Arab conquest of Persia in the 7th century CE. Despite persecution and the decline of Zoroastrian influence, the faith persisted among communities, and Nowruz continued to be celebrated.

2. Zoroastrian Diaspora: Over the centuries, Zoroastrian communities faced migrations and diaspora, particularly to regions like India. Despite challenges, these communities retained their cultural and religious identity, contributing to the global mosaic of Zoroastrianism.

Revival and Cultural Heritage:

1. Contemporary Zoroastrian Communities: Today, Zoroastrian communities exist in various parts of the world, including Iran, India, and diaspora communities. Efforts to preserve and revitalize Zoroastrian traditions contribute to the ongoing cultural heritage associated with Nowruz.

2. Zoroastrian Contributions to Persian Culture: Zoroastrianism has left an indelible mark on Persian culture, influencing art, literature, and philosophy. Nowruz, with its roots in Zoroastrian cosmology, stands as a testament to the enduring legacy of this ancient faith.

Conclusion: Zoroastrian Threads in the Nowruz Tapestry:

As we conclude our exploration of "Zoroastrian History" within the context of Nowruz, the threads of this ancient faith weave seamlessly into the vibrant tapestry of the festival. Zoroastrianism's profound influence on Nowruz is a testament to the enduring power of cultural and spiritual traditions, bridging the past and the present in a celebration that transcends borders and embraces the spirit of renewal.

In the chapters that follow, we will continue our journey through the traditions, customs, and rituals that define Nowruz, unraveling the layers of cultural significance that make it a cherished and universal celebration of new beginnings.

Haft Seen Table Setting: A Symphony of Symbols in Nowruz

As the arrival of spring heralds a season of renewal and hope, the Nowruz celebration comes to life with a vibrant and symbolic display—the Haft Seen table. This intricate tableau, adorned with seven symbolic items starting with the Persian letter "S," holds the essence of Nowruz's cultural richness and Zoroastrian heritage. In this exploration of "Haft Seen Table Setting," we embark on a journey through the layers of meaning woven into each element, unraveling the tapestry of traditions that make this arrangement a central focus of Nowruz festivities.

The Essence of Haft Seen:

1. Numerical Symbolism: The number seven, embodied in the Haft Seen, holds deep cultural and spiritual significance. In Persian culture and Zoroastrianism, the number seven symbolizes completeness, perfection, and the seven creations of Ahura Mazda.

2. Symbolic Letters: Each item on the Haft Seen table begins with the Persian letter "S" (س), adding a linguistic and aesthetic dimension to the arrangement. The repetition of this letter enhances the visual harmony of the display.

3. Nowruz and the Vernal Equinox: The timing of Nowruz, coinciding with the vernal equinox, aligns with the

Zoroastrian concept of the eternal battle between light and darkness. The Haft Seen serves as a manifestation of this cosmic struggle and the triumph of light.

Elements of the Haft Seen:

1. Sabzeh (سبزه): Sprouted Wheat or Barley:

- Symbolism of Growth: Sabzeh represents rebirth and the flourishing of nature. The sprouted grains symbolize the rejuvenation of life and the promise of a new beginning.

- Connection to Zoroastrianism: The emphasis on the growth of greenery reflects Zoroastrian reverence for the natural elements, particularly the earth and its ability to nurture life.

2. Samanu (سمنو): Sweet Pudding:

- Symbol of Power and Strength: Samanu is a sweet and nutritious pudding made from wheat germ. Its richness symbolizes strength, resilience, and the sweetness of life.

- Historical Roots: Samanu's presence on the Haft Seen table connects to ancient traditions, including offerings made in fire temples as a symbol of devotion and strength.

3. Senjed (سنجد): Oleaster Fruit:

- Symbol of Love and Compassion: Senjed, the oleaster fruit, represents love, compassion, and kindness. Its inclusion emphasizes the importance of these virtues in the pursuit of a harmonious and just society.

- Cultural Significance: In Persian poetry and literature, senjed is often used as a metaphor for love, with its sweet taste symbolizing the sweetness of affection.

4. Seer (سیر): Garlic:

- Protective Symbolism: Seer, or garlic, is a symbol of protection against negative forces and illnesses. Its pungent aroma is believed to ward off evil spirits and bring about physical well-being.

- Connection to Zoroastrian Rituals: Garlic has historical ties to Zoroastrian rituals, where it was used in ceremonies to purify and protect individuals from spiritual harm.

5. Seeb (سیب): Apple:

- Symbol of Beauty and Health: Seeb, the apple, represents beauty, good health, and the sweetness of life. Its crispness and natural sweetness symbolize the enjoyment of life's pleasures.

- Historical Roots: Apples have historical significance in Persian culture, with references in literature and art, symbolizing fertility and vitality.

6. Somāq (سماق): Sumac Berries:

- Symbol of Patience and the Sunrise: Somāq, or sumac berries, evoke the colors of the sunrise and symbolize the patience required for the unfolding of a new day. Its tartness represents the challenges that bring balance to life.

- Zoroastrian Connection: Sumac is associated with Zoroastrian rituals, where its use in fire temples is believed to enhance the ritualistic experience.

7. Serkeh (سرکه): Vinegar:

- Symbol of Aging and Wisdom: Serkeh, or vinegar, represents aging and the wisdom that comes with the passage of time. It symbolizes the importance of experience and the lessons learned over the years.

- Zoroastrian Significance: In Zoroastrianism, vinegar is linked to rituals and is considered a purifying substance, reflecting the idea of transforming challenges into wisdom.

Arrangement and Aesthetics:

1. Elegant Display: The arrangement of the Haft Seen is an artful process, with each item carefully placed to create a visually appealing display. The aesthetics reflect Persian cultural values, emphasizing beauty and harmony.

- Color Coordination: Elements are chosen not only for their symbolic meanings but also for their colors. The diverse colors contribute to the vibrancy of the tableau, creating a visual feast.

2. Tablecloth and Decorations: The Haft Seen is typically set on a spread of fabric, often with intricate

patterns and designs. Additional decorations, such as flowers, candles, and traditional items, enhance the overall elegance and festive atmosphere.

Haft Seen and Zoroastrian Spirituality:

1. Alignment with Zoroastrian Principles: The Haft Seen table embodies Zoroastrian principles of purity, balance, and reverence for nature. The elements chosen reflect the interconnectedness of the physical and spiritual realms.

2. Continuity of Zoroastrian Traditions: The Haft Seen serves as a testament to the continuity of Zoroastrian traditions within the context of Nowruz. Elements like sabzeh and samanu harken back to ancient rituals that celebrated the cycle of nature.

Haft Seen Around the World:

1. Global Adaptations: As Nowruz has spread to various parts of the world, the Haft Seen tradition has adapted to local customs and availability of items. Communities globally embrace the core symbolism while incorporating regional variations.

2. Community Participation: The preparation and arrangement of the Haft Seen involve the active participation of families and communities. It fosters a sense of shared

culture and tradition, uniting individuals in the joyous anticipation of the new year.

Educational Significance:

1. Teaching Cultural Values: The Haft Seen serves as a valuable tool for teaching cultural values, traditions, and the historical roots of Nowruz. Educational initiatives aim to convey the rich symbolism to younger generations.

2. Preservation of Heritage: Efforts to preserve Zoroastrian heritage and cultural practices include initiatives to promote the Haft Seen tradition. Cultural events, workshops, and educational programs contribute to the transmission of knowledge.

Conclusion: Haft Seen—A Cultural Masterpiece:

As we conclude our exploration of "Haft Seen Table Setting," the significance of this cultural masterpiece becomes clear. The Haft Seen is not merely a tableau of items; it is a symphony of symbols that resonates with Zoroastrian heritage, Persian culture, and the universal themes of renewal and hope.

In the chapters that follow, we will continue our journey through the traditions, customs, and rituals that define Nowruz, unraveling the layers of cultural significance that make it a cherished and universal celebration of new beginnings.

Out With the Old: Nowruz's Rituals of Purification and Renewal

As the buds of spring unfurl and the vernal equinox marks the onset of a new season, Nowruz invites us to partake in a ritualistic journey—out with the old, and in with the new. This chapter explores the profound significance of Nowruz's "Out With the Old" theme, delving into the rituals and customs that symbolize the purification of the past year, making space for the freshness and potential of the year ahead.

The Concept of Renewal:

1. Philosophy of Renewal: Nowruz embodies a philosophy of constant renewal and rebirth. The festival encapsulates the cyclical nature of life, reflecting the eternal battle between light and darkness—a theme deeply rooted in Zoroastrian cosmology.

2. The Vernal Equinox: Nowruz's alignment with the vernal equinox further emphasizes the theme of renewal. The equinox, when day and night are of equal length, symbolizes balance and heralds the triumph of light over darkness, setting the stage for the journey "out with the old."

Fire Jumping and Chaharshanbe Suri:

1. Cleansing through Fire: The Chaharshanbe Suri, celebrated on the eve of the last Wednesday before Nowruz,

involves a unique ritual—fire jumping. Participants leap over bonfires, a symbolic act of purging themselves of the impurities and misfortunes of the past year.

2. Symbolism of Fire: Fire, a sacred element in Zoroastrianism, holds purification properties. By jumping over the flames, individuals seek not only physical purification but also spiritual cleansing, leaving behind the old and embracing the purity of the new year.

3. Community Participation: Chaharshanbe Suri is a communal celebration, bringing together families and communities. The collective act of fire jumping fosters a sense of unity and shared determination to leave behind the challenges of the past.

Khane Tekani - Shaking the House:

1. Symbolism of House Shaking: Khane Tekani, or "Shaking the House," is a traditional Nowruz activity where families engage in a thorough cleaning of their homes. This goes beyond mere physical cleanliness; it symbolizes the shaking off of accumulated dust, negative energy, and stagnant vibes.

2. Sweeping Out Negativity: The act of sweeping and cleaning is accompanied by the belief that negative energy and misfortune are swept away, making space for positivity and good fortune in the coming year.

3. Preparation for Guests: Beyond personal homes, communities also engage in collective cleaning efforts. Public spaces, parks, and streets are tidied up in anticipation of the gatherings and festivities that characterize Nowruz.

Renewing Wardrobe and Personal Items:

1. New Clothes for the New Year: It is customary for individuals to purchase new clothes for Nowruz, symbolizing a fresh start. Wearing new attire represents the shedding of the old and the embrace of a renewed self as the new year dawns.

2. Repairing and Replacing Possessions: Nowruz is also a time for repairing or replacing worn-out items. This practice extends beyond personal belongings to include the refurbishment of homes and public spaces, contributing to an overall sense of rejuvenation.

3. Donating Unneeded Items: A spirit of generosity is intertwined with the "out with the old" theme. It is common for people to donate items they no longer need, contributing to a sense of community support and sharing.

Forgiveness and Reconciliation:

1. Seeking Forgiveness: Nowruz encourages individuals to engage in acts of forgiveness and reconciliation. It is a time to mend strained relationships, let go of grudges, and start anew with a clean slate.

2. Visiting Elders and Relatives: Making amends often involves visiting elders and relatives, seeking their blessings, and asking for forgiveness for any past transgressions. This tradition strengthens familial bonds and fosters a sense of unity.

3. Symbolic Gesture of Embrace: The act of seeking forgiveness is a symbolic gesture that aligns with Zoroastrian values of compassion and unity. It reflects the belief that a purified heart is essential for embracing the opportunities of the coming year.

Farewell to the Past Year:

1. Reflection and Gratitude: Nowruz encourages introspection, prompting individuals to reflect on the events of the past year. Expressing gratitude for lessons learned and acknowledging personal growth is an integral part of bidding farewell to the old.

2. Burning of "Siyah Chal:" In some traditions, a symbolic structure known as "Siyah Chal" is constructed. This represents the past year, and on the eve of Nowruz, it is set ablaze. The burning symbolizes the release of the past, making way for a new chapter.

3. Letting Go of Regrets: Nowruz invites individuals to release any regrets or burdens carried from the past. The

focus is on embracing the present moment and looking forward to the opportunities that the new year holds.

Transition from Darkness to Light:

1. Bonfires and Light Celebrations: Bonfires and the lighting of candles play a significant role in the "out with the old" theme. These activities symbolize the triumph of light over darkness, echoing Zoroastrian principles of cosmic balance and renewal.

2. Community Gatherings: The lighting of bonfires often takes place in communal spaces, bringing people together. Community members share in the symbolic act of dispelling darkness and welcoming the brightness of the new year.

3. Symbolic Transition: The transition from darkness to light holds metaphorical significance. It represents the journey from challenges and uncertainties to a state of clarity, optimism, and renewed hope.

Conclusion: The Purification and Liberation of Nowruz:

As we conclude our exploration of "Out With the Old" within the context of Nowruz, the profound symbolism of purification and renewal comes into focus. Nowruz's rituals, whether through fire jumping, house shaking, or seeking forgiveness, collectively create a tapestry of traditions that liberate individuals from the burdens of the past.

In the chapters that follow, we will continue our journey through the traditions, customs, and rituals that define Nowruz, unraveling the layers of cultural significance that make it a cherished and universal celebration of new beginnings.

In With the New: Nowruz's Resplendent Beginnings and Symbolic Traditions

As the dawn of spring bathes the world in a gentle glow, Nowruz beckons us to embrace the promise of new beginnings. This chapter explores the enchanting theme of "In With the New" within the tapestry of Nowruz, delving into the symbolic traditions and cultural practices that herald the arrival of the new year with resplendent optimism and hope.

Haft Seen's Symbolic Continuation:

1. Haft Seen Renewed: The Haft Seen, a central feature of Nowruz, takes on a renewed significance as families meticulously arrange and display the seven symbolic items starting with the Persian letter "S." Each element, from Sabzeh (sprouted wheat) to Serkeh (vinegar), carries profound meaning, symbolizing fertility, strength, sweetness, and wisdom.

2. Fresh Additions to Haft Seen: Families often introduce new elements to their Haft Seen table, reflecting personal aspirations and desires for the upcoming year. These additions serve as visual affirmations of hope, growth, and prosperity.

3. Decorative Elements: The Haft Seen tableau is adorned with decorative items such as flowers, candles, and

traditional artifacts. These embellishments not only enhance the aesthetic appeal but also symbolize the beauty and abundance that the new year promises.

Nowruz Cuisine and Culinary Traditions:

1. Feast of Renewal: Nowruz is synonymous with indulgent feasts that celebrate the bounty of the season. Traditional dishes, bursting with flavors and cultural significance, mark the beginning of the new year with culinary delight.

2. Nowruz Specialties: Culinary delights such as Sabzi Polo (herbed rice), Mahi Polo (herbed rice with fish), and Ash-e Reshteh (noodle soup) are staples of Nowruz feasts. Each dish carries symbolic meanings related to abundance, prosperity, and the renewal of life.

3. Sweet Beginnings: Sweets and desserts hold a special place in Nowruz celebrations. Pastries, cookies, and confections, often infused with fragrant spices and nuts, symbolize the sweetness of life and the joy that the new year brings.

Nowruz Shopping and Market Traditions:

1. Bustling Bazaars: In the weeks leading up to Nowruz, markets and bazaars come alive with vibrant colors and the hustle and bustle of shoppers. Families engage in the ritual of purchasing new clothes, home decorations, and

festive items to usher in the new year with a sense of renewal.

2. Goldfish and Plants: Goldfish, representing life and good fortune, are popular purchases during Nowruz. Additionally, the sale of plants and flowers, particularly hyacinths and tulips, contributes to the festive atmosphere and the anticipation of spring's blossoming beauty.

3. Community Connections: Nowruz shopping is not merely a transactional activity; it fosters a sense of community. Families share the excitement of preparing for the festivities, and the exchange of gifts and well-wishes deepens social bonds.

Nowruz Visits and Celebratory Gatherings:

1. Visiting Family and Friends: Nowruz is a time for familial and social connections. Visiting relatives and friends, exchanging gifts, and sharing meals create a sense of community and reinforce the bonds that form the foundation of the new year.

2. Gift-Giving Traditions: Gifts exchanged during Nowruz often hold symbolic meanings. From traditional items to modern tokens of appreciation, the act of giving reflects a desire for prosperity, happiness, and the well-being of loved ones.

3. Nowruz Parties and Events: Communities come together to organize Nowruz parties and events, featuring music, dance, and cultural performances. These gatherings provide a joyous space for people to welcome the new year with festivity and shared enthusiasm.

Nowruz Prayers and Spiritual Renewal:

1. Spiritual Reflection: Nowruz is a time for spiritual introspection and renewal. Individuals engage in prayers and meditative practices to reflect on the past and set positive intentions for the future.

2. Visiting Religious Sites: Many individuals embark on pilgrimages to religious sites and temples during Nowruz, seeking blessings and spiritual guidance for the new year. These visits symbolize a commitment to a spiritual journey and the pursuit of inner peace.

3. Zoroastrian Rituals: For Zoroastrians, Nowruz is deeply connected to Zoroastrian rituals and prayers. Participation in ceremonies at fire temples and the observance of Zoroastrian traditions contribute to the spiritual ambiance of the new year.

Educational and Artistic Renewal:

1. Educational Initiatives: Nowruz provides an opportunity for educational renewal. Schools and cultural institutions organize programs and workshops that highlight

the cultural significance of Nowruz, fostering an understanding and appreciation for diverse traditions.

2. Artistic Expressions: Nowruz inspires artistic expressions that capture the essence of new beginnings. From paintings and sculptures to poetry and music, artists channel the spirit of renewal into creative works that resonate with the themes of hope and optimism.

3. Cultural Performances: The new year is often marked by cultural performances that showcase traditional dances, music, and storytelling. These artistic expressions serve as a vibrant tapestry that reflects the cultural diversity and creativity associated with Nowruz.

Environmental Initiatives and Nature's Renewal:

1. Nowruz and Nature: The festival of Nowruz is intricately linked to the renewal of nature. Planting trees, cleaning natural landscapes, and engaging in environmental initiatives symbolize a commitment to preserving the Earth's beauty and vitality.

2. Symbolism of Flowers and Plants: Flowers and plants play a central role in Nowruz, symbolizing the rebirth of nature. The blooming of hyacinths, tulips, and other spring flowers aligns with the broader theme of new life and growth.

3. Environmental Awareness: Nowruz serves as a platform for promoting environmental consciousness. Initiatives focused on sustainability, waste reduction, and eco-friendly practices align with the ethos of Nowruz and its celebration of a harmonious relationship with the natural world.

Nowruz and Global Communities:

1. Global Celebrations: Nowruz has transcended cultural boundaries, and its celebration is not confined to specific regions. Communities around the world embrace Nowruz, contributing to a global tapestry of shared traditions and renewed aspirations.

2. Diverse Interpretations: The global embrace of Nowruz has led to diverse interpretations and adaptations of its traditions. Communities from different cultural backgrounds infuse their unique flavors into Nowruz celebrations while honoring the festival's universal themes.

3. Unity in Diversity: Nowruz exemplifies the beauty of unity in diversity. Regardless of cultural differences, the festival brings people together in a shared celebration of new beginnings, fostering understanding and appreciation for the richness of global traditions.

Conclusion: Nowruz's Radiant Dawn of New Beginnings:

As we conclude our exploration of "In With the New" within the context of Nowruz, the resplendent dawn of new beginnings comes into focus. Nowruz's traditions, whether expressed through the Haft Seen, culinary delights, festive gatherings, or spiritual reflections, collectively create an atmosphere of optimism and hope as individuals and communities welcome the new year with open hearts.

In the chapters that follow, we will continue our journey through the traditions, customs, and rituals that define Nowruz, unraveling the layers of cultural significance that make it a cherished and universal celebration of new beginnings.

Chapter 7: Hijri New Year

Islamic Calendar: Navigating Time with the Lunar Tapestry

In the vast tapestry of time, the Islamic calendar stands as a unique and sacred chronicle, guiding the Muslim community through the rhythm of lunar phases and celestial cycles. This chapter explores the intricacies of the Islamic calendar, a lustrous thread woven into the fabric of Islamic culture, spirituality, and daily life.

The Lunar Foundation:

1. Lunar Calculations: At the heart of the Islamic calendar lies the lunar system, where months are determined by the cycles of the moon. Unlike the solar-based Gregorian calendar, the Islamic calendar is a lunar calendar, aligning with the astronomical movements of the moon.

2. 12 Lunar Months: The Islamic calendar comprises 12 lunar months, each beginning with the sighting of the new crescent moon. These months are alternately 29 or 30 days long, resulting in a total of 354 or 355 days in a year. The lunar calendar thus embarks on a continuous journey through the celestial expanse.

3. Hijra: A Pivotal Moment: The Islamic calendar begins with a momentous event—the Hijra, the migration of Prophet Muhammad (peace be upon him) from Mecca to

Medina in 622 CE. The inception of the Islamic calendar marks the start of a new era, emphasizing the significance of Hijra in Islamic history.

Names of the Months:

1. Sacred Significance: Each month in the Islamic calendar carries its own spiritual significance, and certain months are considered especially sacred. For example, Ramadan, the month of fasting, holds a central place, while Dhul-Hijjah is the month of pilgrimage during Hajj.

2. Muharram: The Sacred Beginning: The Islamic year commences with the month of Muharram. Considered one of the four sacred months, Muharram holds historical and religious importance, with the 10th day, known as Ashura, being a day of fasting and reflection.

3. Dhul-Hijjah: The Pilgrimage Month: The last month of the Islamic calendar, Dhul-Hijjah, witnesses the pilgrimage to Mecca, known as Hajj. The annual pilgrimage is a pillar of Islam, and the days of Hajj are imbued with profound spiritual significance.

Alignment with Lunar Phases:

1. Crescent Moon Sighting: The sighting of the crescent moon marks the beginning of each Islamic month. This tradition emphasizes the visual confirmation of the

moon, fostering community involvement and a sense of shared religious observance.

2. Unity in Moon Sighting: The practice of moon sighting promotes unity within the Muslim community. Communities around the world come together to witness the new moon, reinforcing a global sense of connection and shared adherence to the lunar calendar.

3. Regional Variations: While the sighting of the crescent moon is a unifying practice, regional variations in moon sighting exist. Different communities may follow local sighting traditions, leading to the celebration of Islamic events on slightly different days.

Flexibility of the Islamic Calendar:

1. Adjusting to Lunar Phases: The lunar calendar is flexible and adapts to the natural cycles of the moon. The variability of lunar months allows for adjustments based on celestial observations, aligning Islamic months with the actual lunar phases.

2. Solar and Lunar Harmony: The Islamic calendar maintains a harmonious relationship with both the lunar and solar systems. While the lunar months define the religious calendar, the solar calendar is also considered for agricultural and financial matters.

3. Leap Years: To synchronize with the solar calendar, the Islamic calendar incorporates an adjustment known as the leap year (intercalation). This additional day ensures that Islamic months continue to align with the seasons over a long period.

Significance of the Islamic Calendar:

1. Religious Observances: The Islamic calendar plays a central role in determining religious observances and rituals. Key events, such as Ramadan, Eid al-Fitr, and Hajj, are intricately tied to specific lunar months, fostering a cyclical and spiritually meaningful journey throughout the year.

2. Birthdays and Anniversaries: Muslims often reference the Islamic calendar for birthdays and anniversaries. The Hijri date of birth is noted with reverence, and significant life events are often marked by reference to the lunar calendar.

3. Commemorating Historical Events: Historical events in Islamic history, such as the Battle of Badr or the Treaty of Hudaybiyyah, are commemorated based on the Hijri calendar. This connection to historical milestones fosters a sense of continuity and reverence for the past.

Challenges and Controversies:

1. Moon Sighting Controversies: The method of moon sighting has been a source of occasional controversy within

the Muslim community. Differences in moon sighting criteria and regional variations have led to debates about the start of Islamic months.

2. Globalization and Standardization: In the modern era, with globalization and technological advancements, there are discussions about standardizing moon sighting practices globally. Some argue for a unified approach to determine the beginning of Islamic months to minimize confusion.

3. Use of Calculations: While traditional moon sighting remains significant, some scholars advocate for the use of astronomical calculations to determine the start of Islamic months. This approach seeks to combine scientific precision with religious observance.

Conclusion: Navigating Time with Lunar Grace:

In conclusion, the Islamic calendar stands as a testament to the graceful navigation of time within the Muslim community. Its lunar tapestry weaves together religious observances, historical commemorations, and personal milestones, offering a unique and sacred rhythm to the lives of millions. As we delve deeper into the Hijri New Year, we will explore the celestial celebrations and spiritual reflections that mark this auspicious moment in the Islamic calendar.

Crescent Moon Sighting: Illuminating the Islamic Calendar

In the celestial ballet that guides the Islamic calendar, the delicate crescent moon takes center stage, casting its ethereal glow to signal the beginning of each lunar month. This chapter explores the intricate art of crescent moon sighting, a tradition that unites the Muslim community in the visual affirmation of time and spiritual observance.

The Significance of the Crescent Moon:

1. Symbol of Renewal: The crescent moon is an emblem of renewal and rebirth in Islamic symbolism. Its slender, illuminated arc represents the beginning of a new lunar month, signaling a fresh cycle of religious observances, prayers, and communal activities.

2. Allah's Creation: The Quranic verses and teachings of Prophet Muhammad (peace be upon him) highlight the celestial wonders as signs of Allah's creation. The sighting of the crescent moon is a tangible manifestation of the divine order, a recurring miracle that resonates with believers.

3. Unity in Observation: Crescent moon sighting fosters a sense of unity within the Muslim community. Regardless of geographical locations or cultural differences, Muslims around the world engage in the shared experience

of observing the crescent moon to commence religious months and festivities.

The Methodology of Crescent Moon Sighting:

1. Naked Eye Observation: Traditionally, crescent moon sighting is conducted with the naked eye. Scholars and community members gather in open spaces to visually confirm the presence of the new moon shortly after sunset. This method aligns with the simplicity of Prophet Muhammad's guidance.

2. Local and Global Perspectives: Moon sighting is often a local affair, with communities relying on visual confirmation within their region. However, globalization and technological advancements have led to discussions about the potential for global moon sighting to standardize the beginning of Islamic months.

3. Community Involvement: Crescent moon sighting is a communal activity that engages people of all ages. Families, scholars, and individuals come together, either physically or through technological means, to witness the sighting, emphasizing the communal nature of Islamic rituals.

Factors Influencing Moon Sighting:

1. Lunar Visibility: The visibility of the crescent moon is influenced by various factors, including atmospheric

conditions, altitude, and the age of the moon. A thin, young moon is more challenging to observe than a slightly older crescent.

2. Geographical Location: The geography of a region plays a crucial role in moon sighting. The angle at which the moon sets after the sun, known as the elongation, varies with location. Therefore, crescent moon sightings may occur on different days in different regions.

3. Technological Aids: While traditional moon sighting relies on visual observation, technological aids such as telescopes and astronomical calculations have become tools for determining the birth of the new moon. However, their usage remains a subject of discussion within the Muslim community.

The Spiritual Journey of Moon Sighting:

1. Anticipation and Excitement: The days leading up to the new month are filled with anticipation and excitement within the Muslim community. Families and individuals eagerly await the announcement of the crescent moon sighting, heralding the commencement of religious activities.

2. Prayers and Reflection: Moon sighting is not only a visual confirmation but also a spiritual experience. Muslims engage in prayers, supplications, and moments of reflection

as they await the sighting, fostering a connection with the divine and a sense of gratitude for the passing of time.

3. Announcement and Celebration: Once the crescent moon is sighted, announcements are made, and communities come alive with celebrations. Mosques, homes, and public spaces are adorned, marking the beginning of the new month with a palpable sense of joy and spiritual fulfillment.

Challenges and Controversies:

1. Differing Opinions: Crescent moon sighting has been a source of differing opinions within the Muslim community. Some scholars emphasize local sightings, while others advocate for a unified global approach. These differences contribute to occasional controversies regarding the start of Islamic months.

2. Technological vs. Visual Sighting: The use of technological aids, such as telescopes and astronomical calculations, has sparked debates. While some argue for the precision and objectivity of these tools, others emphasize the simplicity and communal nature of visual sightings.

3. Community Engagement: Moon sighting involves the engagement of the community, and disagreements on the methodology can lead to fragmentation. Efforts to foster

unity in moon sighting practices continue to be a topic of discussion among scholars and religious authorities.

Modern Challenges and Solutions:

1. Globalization and Standardization: In an era of globalization, discussions about global moon sighting and standardization persist. Efforts to streamline moon sighting practices globally aim to minimize confusion and foster unity within the Muslim community.

2. Technology and Transparency: Technological advancements have led to the development of apps and websites that provide real-time information about moon sightings. These tools enhance transparency and allow individuals to track lunar phases, contributing to a more informed and engaged community.

3. Educational Initiatives: Addressing the challenges associated with moon sighting involves educational initiatives. Community leaders and scholars strive to educate the public about the factors influencing moon sighting, the diversity of opinions, and the importance of unity in religious observances.

Conclusion: Crescent Moon, Shared Witness:

As we conclude our exploration of crescent moon sighting, the radiant arc of the new moon stands as a symbol of shared witness within the Muslim community. In the chapters that follow, we will delve deeper into the celebrations and rituals that mark the Hijri New Year, exploring the spiritual reflections and communal activities that unfold under the luminous guidance of the crescent moon.

Reflection and Atonement: Embracing Spiritual Renewal

In the sacred embrace of the Hijri New Year, Muslims embark on a profound journey of reflection and atonement. This chapter delves into the spiritual significance of this period, exploring the practices and rituals that mark a time of deep introspection, repentance, and the pursuit of spiritual renewal.

The Sacred Transition:

1. The Hijri New Year: As the Islamic calendar transitions to a new year, Muslims engage in a sacred pause for reflection. This moment is not merely the flipping of a calendar page but a symbolic journey into a space of spiritual contemplation and growth.

2. A Time for Renewal: The Hijri New Year represents an opportunity for Muslims to renew their commitment to faith, aligning their lives with the teachings of Islam. This period fosters a sense of spiritual rejuvenation, encouraging believers to draw closer to Allah.

3. Aligning with Hijra: The beginning of the Islamic calendar with the Hijra emphasizes the transformative journey of Prophet Muhammad (peace be upon him). Believers are inspired to reflect on their own life journeys,

seeking alignment with the principles of Hijra—perseverance, resilience, and unwavering faith.

The Essence of Reflection:

1. Contemplating Life's Journey: Muslims use the Hijri New Year as an opportunity for introspection. Reflecting on personal achievements, challenges, and the overall journey of faith allows individuals to gain insights into their spiritual growth.

2. Gratitude for Blessings: Reflection involves expressing gratitude for the blessings received. Believers take stock of the past year, acknowledging Allah's mercy, guidance, and provisions, fostering a sense of humility and thankfulness.

3. Learning from Challenges: Difficulties and trials are inevitable in life. The Hijri New Year prompts believers to reflect on challenges as opportunities for growth, resilience, and the development of patience and perseverance.

Practices of Reflection:

1. Extended Prayers and Duas: During the Hijri New Year, Muslims engage in extended prayers and supplications, seeking guidance, forgiveness, and blessings for the coming year. These intimate conversations with Allah serve as a cornerstone for personal reflection.

2. Journaling and Self-Examination: Some individuals find solace in journaling, using the written word as a means of self-examination. Recording thoughts, feelings, and spiritual goals allows for a tangible expression of one's inner journey.

3. Retreats and Spiritual Seclusion: Engaging in periods of retreat or spiritual seclusion is a practice embraced by some Muslims. Whether at home or in designated retreat centers, individuals withdraw from the noise of daily life to focus on spiritual reflection and connection with Allah.

Atonement and Seeking Forgiveness:

1. Repentance (Tawbah): A central theme during the Hijri New Year is repentance. Muslims recognize their shortcomings and sins, turning sincerely to Allah in repentance. Tawbah involves acknowledging mistakes, feeling remorse, and committing to positive change.

2. Seeking Forgiveness: Believers seek forgiveness not only from Allah but also from fellow human beings. Resolving conflicts, seeking pardon, and extending forgiveness contribute to a harmonious and spiritually cleansed community.

3. Rituals of Forgiveness: Some families and communities engage in specific rituals symbolizing

forgiveness. Acts such as communal prayers, breaking fast together, and exchanging gifts become expressions of mutual forgiveness and unity.

The Day of Arafah and Eid al-Adha:

1. Arafah Day Fasting: The 9th day of the Islamic month of Dhul-Hijjah, known as the Day of Arafah, holds immense significance. Fasting on this day is believed to expiate sins of the past and coming year, offering a unique opportunity for atonement.

2. Eid al-Adha and Sacrifice: The culmination of the Hajj pilgrimage brings forth Eid al-Adha, the Festival of Sacrifice. Beyond the rituals of animal sacrifice, this occasion symbolizes the willingness to sacrifice for Allah and the importance of self-discipline.

3. Community Celebrations: Eid al-Adha is a time of joy and communal celebration. Families come together, share meals, and engage in acts of charity, embodying the spirit of sacrifice and gratitude.

Acts of Charity and Service:

1. Zakat and Sadaqah: The Hijri New Year inspires acts of charity and generosity. Muslims fulfill their financial obligations through Zakat and engage in voluntary giving (Sadaqah) to support those in need, contributing to the welfare of the community.

2. Community Service: Volunteering and community service are expressions of gratitude and atonement. Muslims actively participate in initiatives that benefit the less fortunate, fostering a sense of social responsibility and compassion.

3. Visiting the Sick and Elderly: Compassion extends to personal interactions, with Muslims visiting the sick, elderly, and those in need. These acts of kindness serve as tangible expressions of the values upheld during the Hijri New Year.

Educational Programs and Lectures:

1. Spiritual Talks and Lectures: Mosques and Islamic centers organize educational programs and lectures during the Hijri New Year. Scholars and community leaders share insights on repentance, reflection, and spiritual growth, guiding believers on their journey of faith.

2. Workshops on Personal Development: Some communities arrange workshops focused on personal development and spiritual growth. Topics may include effective goal-setting, time management, and strategies for maintaining a balance between worldly and spiritual pursuits.

3. Youth Engagement Programs: Special programs for youth provide spaces for reflection tailored to their unique

experiences and challenges. Interactive sessions, discussions, and activities encourage young Muslims to connect with the spiritual dimensions of the new year.

Challenges and Opportunities:

1. Balancing Spiritual and Mundane Obligations: In the contemporary world, Muslims face the challenge of balancing spiritual obligations with the demands of daily life. The Hijri New Year offers an opportunity to reassess priorities and find harmony between worldly and spiritual pursuits.

2. Addressing Mental Health: The reflective nature of the Hijri New Year brings attention to mental health considerations. Communities increasingly recognize the importance of addressing mental well-being, fostering support systems, and providing resources for those in need.

3. Navigating Cultural Practices: Cultural practices surrounding the Hijri New Year vary. Muslims navigate the challenge of distinguishing between authentic religious traditions and cultural customs, aiming to ensure that the essence of reflection and atonement remains at the forefront.

Conclusion: The Tapestry of Spiritual Renewal:

As we conclude our exploration of "Reflection and Atonement" within the context of the Hijri New Year, the tapestry of spiritual renewal comes into focus. This period of deep introspection, repentance, and seeking forgiveness serves as a guiding light, illuminating the path towards a more spiritually aligned and purposeful life. In the ensuing chapters, we will continue our journey through the traditions and celebrations that define the Hijri New Year, unraveling the layers of cultural significance that make it a cherished and universal celebration of new beginnings.

Celebrations and Charity: Communal Joy and Compassionate Giving

As the Hijri New Year dawns, Muslims around the world come together in joyous celebration and charitable endeavors, creating a tapestry of communal unity and compassionate giving. This chapter explores the vibrant festivities and acts of charity that define the essence of the Hijri New Year, showcasing the shared humanity and benevolence that mark this auspicious occasion.

Communal Celebrations:

1. Decorating Homes and Mosques: The arrival of the Hijri New Year is met with a burst of colors and decorations. Homes and mosques are adorned with banners, lights, and festive ornaments, creating an atmosphere of joy and anticipation.

2. Special Congregational Prayers: The Hijri New Year is marked by special congregational prayers held in mosques and Islamic centers. These prayers are moments of reflection, gratitude, and supplication, bringing the community together in a shared spiritual experience.

3. Community Gatherings and Events: Muslims gather in community halls, public spaces, and homes to celebrate the Hijri New Year. Cultural performances, poetry recitations, and storytelling sessions contribute to a festive

ambiance that transcends geographical and cultural boundaries.

Feasting and Sharing Meals:

1. Special New Year's Meals: Families come together to prepare and share special meals, symbolizing abundance and gratitude. Traditional dishes, sweets, and festive treats become an integral part of the New Year's celebration.

2. Community Potlucks and Feasts: Communities organize potluck dinners and communal feasts where families contribute dishes to share with neighbors and those in need. These events foster a sense of camaraderie and unity.

3. Symbolism in Food: Certain foods hold symbolic significance during the Hijri New Year. Dates, for example, are often included in meals, representing blessings and the traditions of the Prophet Muhammad (peace be upon him).

Charitable Acts and Sadaqah:

1. Zakat Al-Fitr: The Hijri New Year is a time for Muslims to fulfill their religious obligation of Zakat al-Fitr. This charitable giving, typically done before Eid al-Fitr, aims to purify those who fast from any indecent act or speech and to help the poor and needy.

2. Community Charity Drives: Mosques and community organizations organize charity drives during the

Hijri New Year, collecting donations for various causes. These initiatives range from providing meals to the less fortunate to supporting education and healthcare projects.

3. Acts of Sadaqah: Beyond the obligatory Zakat, Muslims engage in voluntary acts of charity, or Sadaqah, during the Hijri New Year. This can include financial contributions, donating goods, or offering one's time and skills to help those in need.

Gift-Giving and Acts of Kindness:

1. Exchanging Gifts: Gift-giving is a cherished tradition during the Hijri New Year. Families and friends exchange presents as expressions of love and goodwill, fostering a sense of generosity and thoughtfulness.

2. Acts of Kindness: The New Year prompts Muslims to engage in acts of kindness and compassion. Simple gestures, such as helping neighbors, visiting the sick, and offering assistance to those facing challenges, become integral to the spirit of the occasion.

3. Supporting Orphanages and Shelters: Communities often direct their charitable efforts toward supporting orphanages, shelters, and other institutions that care for the vulnerable. Providing essentials, organizing events, and offering emotional support contribute to the welfare of those in need.

Educational and Cultural Programs:

1. Islamic Lectures and Workshops: Mosques and educational institutions host lectures and workshops during the Hijri New Year, focusing on themes of gratitude, compassion, and community building. These events contribute to the spiritual and intellectual enrichment of the community.

2. Cultural Exhibitions: Cultural exhibitions showcasing Islamic art, literature, and history add a creative dimension to the celebrations. These exhibitions serve as platforms for learning, appreciation, and the exchange of cultural knowledge.

3. Children's Programs: Special programs for children are organized, incorporating educational activities, storytelling sessions, and arts and crafts. These initiatives instill a sense of cultural pride and religious understanding in the younger generation.

Challenges and Opportunities:

1. Ensuring Inclusivity: In multicultural societies, Muslims navigate the challenge of ensuring that celebrations are inclusive and respectful of diverse cultural backgrounds within the Muslim community. Efforts to embrace cultural diversity enrich the tapestry of the celebrations.

2. Balancing Festivities with Reflection: Amidst the joyous celebrations, Muslims aim to strike a balance between festive activities and moments of reflection. The challenge lies in ensuring that the essence of the occasion, including gratitude and spiritual growth, remains at the forefront.

3. Addressing Economic Disparities: The Hijri New Year prompts reflection on economic disparities within Muslim communities. Addressing issues of poverty and inequality becomes an opportunity for collective action and sustainable change.

Conclusion: A Tapestry of Shared Joy and Compassion:

As we conclude our exploration of "Celebrations and Charity" within the context of the Hijri New Year, a vibrant tapestry of shared joy and compassionate giving unfolds. This auspicious occasion brings communities together in festive celebration, fostering a spirit of generosity and unity. In the chapters that follow, we will continue our journey through the diverse traditions and rituals that define the Hijri New Year, unraveling the layers of cultural significance that make it a cherished and universal celebration of new beginnings.

Conclusion
Finding Unity in Diversity

As we draw the curtain on our exploration of the myriad traditions and celebrations surrounding the Hijri New Year, the overarching theme that emerges is that of finding unity in diversity. This concluding chapter delves into the rich tapestry woven by the various cultures, customs, and rituals, highlighting the shared humanity that unites Muslims across the globe during this auspicious occasion.

Celebrating Diversity:

1. Cultural Variations: The beauty of the Hijri New Year lies in the diverse ways it is celebrated across cultures. From the colorful lights adorning homes during Diwali to the rhythmic water splashes of Songkran, each cultural expression adds a unique thread to the global tapestry of celebrations.

2. Symbolism and Significance: The diversity of rituals and customs is not merely a reflection of cultural differences but a testament to the richness of human expression. Whether it's the crescent moon sighting in diverse locales or the symbolic foods shared among families, each tradition carries profound meanings and deep-rooted symbolism.

3. Shared Values: Beneath the surface of cultural diversity lies a bedrock of shared values. The emphasis on

gratitude, reflection, charity, and unity during the Hijri New Year serves as a common thread that weaves through the various celebrations. This shared ethos transcends borders and languages, connecting Muslims in a shared spiritual journey.

Common Themes Across Cultures:

1. Light and Illumination: Many New Year celebrations revolve around the theme of light. Whether it's the sparkling fireworks of Diwali, the glow of lanterns in Chinese New Year, or the symbolic lighting of candles during Nowruz, the shared emphasis on illuminating darkness symbolizes hope, positivity, and the pursuit of a brighter future.

2. Renewal and Fresh Starts: Across cultures, the New Year signifies a time of renewal. Whether it's the turning of the lunar calendar in the Hijri New Year, the commencement of spring in Nowruz, or the beginning of a new agricultural cycle in Songkran, there's a collective aspiration for fresh starts, growth, and positive change.

3. Prayers for Prosperity: A common thread woven into the fabric of New Year celebrations is the universal prayer for prosperity. Whether expressed through the rhythmic beats of the Joya No Kane bell ringing in Japan or the poignant sound of the shofar during Rosh Hashanah, the

shared yearning for abundance and blessings echoes across diverse cultures.

Challenges and Opportunities in Diversity:

1. Navigating Cultural Sensitivities: Celebrating diversity comes with the responsibility of navigating cultural sensitivities. Muslims globally grapple with the challenge of honoring diverse traditions while ensuring that the essence of Islamic teachings remains at the heart of the celebrations.

2. Addressing Misconceptions: The diversity of New Year celebrations offers an opportunity to dispel misconceptions and foster understanding. Educational initiatives and intercultural dialogues can bridge gaps, promoting a more nuanced and accurate understanding of the cultural and religious significance of these celebrations.

3. Building Bridges Across Communities: The Hijri New Year serves as a bridge between Muslims and non-Muslims, providing a platform for cultural exchange and dialogue. Community events, open houses, and educational programs create spaces where people from different backgrounds can come together, fostering mutual respect and understanding.

Carrying Traditions Into Future Generations:

1. Passing Down Cultural Heritage: The transmission of cultural traditions from one generation to the next is a

vital aspect of preserving heritage. Families play a crucial role in passing down the customs, stories, and rituals associated with the New Year, ensuring that the cultural tapestry remains vibrant and relevant.

2. Educational Initiatives: Schools, mosques, and community organizations contribute to the preservation of cultural traditions through educational initiatives. Workshops, classes, and cultural programs empower younger generations with the knowledge and understanding of the significance behind New Year celebrations.

3. Innovation and Adaptation: As societies evolve, the challenge lies in balancing tradition with innovation. Finding creative ways to adapt cultural practices to contemporary contexts ensures that New Year celebrations remain dynamic and resonate with the evolving needs of diverse communities.

Celebrating Our Shared Humanity:

1. Beyond Religious Boundaries: The celebrations surrounding the Hijri New Year offer a glimpse into the shared humanity that transcends religious boundaries. Muslims and non-Muslims alike participate in the festivities, recognizing the universal themes of hope, renewal, and the pursuit of a better future.

2. Interfaith Understanding: The diversity of New Year celebrations provides an opportunity for interfaith understanding. Open dialogues and collaborative events foster connections between people of different faiths, breaking down barriers and building bridges based on shared values.

3. Global Solidarity: In a world often marked by division, New Year celebrations exemplify moments of global solidarity. Whether it's communities coming together to support charitable causes or individuals extending gestures of kindness across cultural lines, these celebrations become powerful symbols of unity.

Conclusion: A Shared Tapestry, A Collective Journey:

As we conclude our journey through the diverse traditions and celebrations of the Hijri New Year, the tapestry that emerges is one of shared joy, compassion, and unity. The cultural variations, customs, and rituals, while diverse, are threads in a larger fabric that binds humanity together. The Hijri New Year becomes a canvas where diverse colors blend harmoniously, creating a masterpiece that reflects the shared aspirations and common humanity of people across the globe. As we step into the future, may this tapestry continue to evolve, telling a story of resilience, understanding, and the enduring beauty of diversity.

Carrying Traditions Into Future Generations

As we stand at the crossroads of the present and the future, the significance of carrying traditions into future generations takes center stage. This concluding chapter delves into the intricate tapestry of passing down the cultural and spiritual heritage associated with the Hijri New Year, exploring the challenges, opportunities, and strategies that ensure these rich traditions endure and thrive in the hands of those yet to come.

The Importance of Passing Down Traditions:

1. Preserving Cultural Identity: The traditions surrounding the Hijri New Year are integral to the cultural identity of Muslim communities. Passing down these traditions becomes a means of preserving a rich and diverse heritage that spans centuries, connecting generations to their roots.

2. Cultural Continuity: The transmission of traditions is a form of cultural continuity. It ensures that the practices, stories, and rituals associated with the New Year remain relevant and meaningful, creating a bridge between the past, present, and future.

3. Spiritual Legacy: Beyond cultural significance, the traditions of the Hijri New Year hold profound spiritual value. Passing down these traditions becomes a way of

nurturing a spiritual legacy, instilling a sense of connection to faith and fostering a deep understanding of Islamic teachings.

Family as the Custodian of Traditions:

1. Role of Elders and Ancestors: Within families, elders and ancestors play a pivotal role in preserving and passing down traditions. Their experiences, stories, and firsthand knowledge become invaluable resources for younger generations seeking to understand the cultural and spiritual dimensions of the New Year celebrations.

2. Oral Tradition and Storytelling: Oral tradition, including storytelling, serves as a powerful method of passing down traditions. Through narratives and anecdotes, elders can share the historical and cultural context of New Year celebrations, creating a living tapestry of shared experiences.

3. Family Rituals and Customs: Families often have unique rituals and customs associated with the Hijri New Year. These may include special prayers, festive meals, and acts of charity. Establishing and maintaining these family traditions contribute to a sense of continuity and belonging.

Educational Initiatives and Community Involvement:

1. Incorporating Traditions in Education: Educational institutions, including Islamic schools and community

centers, play a crucial role in passing down traditions. Integrating teachings about the cultural and religious significance of the Hijri New Year into curricula ensures that younger generations are educated about their heritage.

2. Community Workshops and Programs: Community organizations can organize workshops and programs focused on the traditions of the Hijri New Year. These events provide platforms for intergenerational dialogue, where elders share their knowledge, and the youth actively engage in learning and embracing their cultural heritage.

3. Mentorship Programs: Establishing mentorship programs within communities creates opportunities for the transfer of knowledge from elders to younger individuals. Elders can serve as mentors, guiding the next generation in understanding, appreciating, and perpetuating the traditions associated with the New Year.

Utilizing Technology for Preservation:

1. Digital Archives and Documentation: In the age of technology, digital archives and documentation become essential tools for preserving traditions. Creating digital repositories of stories, images, and videos related to the Hijri New Year ensures that this cultural heritage is not lost to time.

2. Interactive Apps and Platforms: Developing interactive apps and online platforms that engage younger generations in learning about the New Year traditions can be effective. These tools can incorporate multimedia elements, quizzes, and interactive experiences to make the learning process engaging and accessible.

3. Social Media and Community Engagement: Leveraging social media for community engagement allows for the widespread sharing of traditions. Community groups, blogs, and social media channels become spaces where individuals can share their experiences, ask questions, and participate in discussions about the Hijri New Year.

Balancing Tradition and Adaptation:

1. Respecting Core Values: While adaptation is essential for traditions to remain relevant, respecting core values is paramount. Balancing innovation with the preservation of fundamental principles ensures that the essence of the Hijri New Year traditions is maintained.

2. Incorporating Contemporary Elements: Integrating contemporary elements into the celebration of the Hijri New Year can make traditions more relatable to younger generations. This may include incorporating modern forms of art, music, or interactive activities while staying true to the cultural and religious significance.

3. Encouraging Active Participation: Actively involving younger generations in the planning and execution of New Year celebrations fosters a sense of ownership. When individuals feel connected to the traditions, they are more likely to carry them forward with enthusiasm and authenticity.

Facing Challenges and Nurturing Growth:

1. Addressing Generational Gaps: One challenge in passing down traditions is the potential gap between generations. Understanding the perspectives of both older and younger individuals allows for open communication and a collaborative approach to preserving traditions.

2. Adapting to Changing Lifestyles: The fast-paced nature of contemporary life presents challenges in maintaining traditional practices. Adapting these practices to fit into changing lifestyles ensures that they remain practical and feasible for future generations.

3. Fostering Inclusivity: As Muslim communities become increasingly diverse, fostering inclusivity is crucial in passing down traditions. Embracing the variety of cultural backgrounds within the community ensures that traditions are respectful and relevant to all.

Conclusion: Sustaining the Flame of Tradition:

As we conclude our exploration into "Carrying Traditions Into Future Generations," the flame of tradition stands illuminated, passed down from elders to the youth, creating a bridge between the past and the future. The Hijri New Year, with its rich tapestry of cultural and spiritual celebrations, holds the promise of enduring through generations. It is not merely a reflection of times past but a living legacy that evolves and adapts, ensuring that the values and traditions associated with this auspicious occasion continue to thrive and resonate in the hearts of those who will carry them forward. In this delicate dance between tradition and the evolving present, the flame is sustained, casting a warm glow onto the path that stretches ahead. May the Hijri New Year, with all its cultural and spiritual richness, continue to guide, inspire, and unite generations yet to come.

Celebrating Our Shared Humanity

As we bring our journey through the diverse traditions and celebrations of the Hijri New Year to a close, a resonant theme emerges — the celebration of our shared humanity. This concluding chapter delves into the universal threads that weave through the rich tapestry of New Year celebrations, transcending cultural, geographical, and religious boundaries. It explores the profound ways in which the Hijri New Year becomes a celebration that unites rather than divides, fostering a sense of interconnectedness that extends far beyond the confines of individual communities.

The Universal Language of Celebration:

1. Beyond Religious Boundaries: The celebration of the Hijri New Year extends an invitation that goes beyond the realm of religious boundaries. While rooted in Islamic tradition, the festivities resonate with people from diverse faiths and cultural backgrounds, creating spaces for shared joy and understanding.

2. Global Participation: The Hijri New Year is not confined to specific regions or nations. Muslims and non-Muslims alike participate in the celebrations, emphasizing the global nature of the occasion. Community events, open houses, and interfaith initiatives become avenues for diverse communities to come together.

3. Embracing Cultural Diversity: The celebrations surrounding the Hijri New Year provide a unique opportunity to embrace and appreciate cultural diversity. From the vibrancy of Diwali to the solemnity of Rosh Hashanah, each cultural expression becomes a brushstroke on the canvas of humanity's collective celebration of new beginnings.

Shared Themes Across Cultures:

1. Light and Illumination: The theme of light is a beacon that guides celebrations across cultures. Whether it's the lantern-lit streets during Diwali, the glow of fireworks in Chinese New Year, or the symbolic lighting of candles in Nowruz, the universal symbolism of light as a metaphor for hope and positivity shines brightly.

2. Renewal and Fresh Starts: New Year celebrations universally symbolize a time of renewal and fresh beginnings. The turning of the lunar calendar in the Hijri New Year, the arrival of spring in Nowruz, or the commencement of a new agricultural cycle in Songkran — each marks a collective aspiration for positive change and growth.

3. Prayers for Prosperity: The universal human desire for prosperity and blessings is a common thread that runs through New Year celebrations. Whether expressed through

the poignant sound of the shofar during Rosh Hashanah or the rhythmic beats of the Joya No Kane bell ringing in Japan, the shared yearning for abundance unites diverse cultures.

Interfaith Understanding and Harmony:

1. Bridging Faith Communities: The celebrations of the Hijri New Year become bridges between faith communities. Interfaith dialogues, joint celebrations, and collaborative initiatives foster understanding and harmony, breaking down barriers that may exist between different religious traditions.

2. Learning from Each Other: The diverse New Year celebrations provide opportunities for mutual learning. Experiencing the customs and rituals of other cultures cultivates appreciation and respect, encouraging individuals to find common ground and celebrate the shared values that underpin these celebrations.

3. Promoting Peaceful Coexistence: The Hijri New Year, with its emphasis on unity and compassion, becomes a catalyst for promoting peaceful coexistence. Communities that celebrate together are more likely to appreciate the richness of diversity, fostering an environment where differences are embraced rather than feared.

Acts of Kindness and Charity:

1. Global Solidarity in Charity: The charitable aspects of the Hijri New Year, such as Zakat al-Fitr, resonate with the global human spirit. Acts of kindness, generosity, and support for those in need become universal languages that transcend cultural and linguistic differences.

2. Community Engagement for Social Causes: Hijri New Year celebrations often involve community engagement in social causes. Whether it's supporting local initiatives, contributing to charitable drives, or participating in community service, these actions exemplify the shared commitment to making a positive impact on society.

3. Building Bridges Through Charity: Acts of charity become bridges that connect individuals and communities. The Hijri New Year provides a platform for building these bridges, encouraging people to reach out across cultural and religious lines to address common challenges and contribute to the well-being of humanity.

Challenges and Opportunities in Diversity:

1. Navigating Cultural Sensitivities: Celebrating diversity comes with the responsibility of navigating cultural sensitivities. Understanding and respecting the cultural nuances within the Muslim community and beyond contribute to creating inclusive celebrations that honor the richness of human expression.

2. Addressing Misconceptions: New Year celebrations offer opportunities to dispel misconceptions and stereotypes. Engaging in open dialogue, educational initiatives, and cultural exchange helps break down barriers, fostering a more accurate understanding of diverse traditions.

3. Fostering Inclusivity: In multicultural societies, fostering inclusivity is crucial for New Year celebrations to resonate with all members of the community. Embracing the variety of cultural backgrounds ensures that celebrations are respectful, inclusive, and reflective of the diverse tapestry of humanity.

Global Unity in Diversity:

1. Beyond Tolerance to Acceptance: The Hijri New Year celebrations prompt a shift from mere tolerance to genuine acceptance. Communities that actively engage with and embrace the diverse expressions of the New Year move beyond surface-level understanding, cultivating a deeper appreciation for the rich mosaic of humanity.

2. Interconnectedness in a Globalized World: In an increasingly globalized world, the Hijri New Year becomes a symbol of interconnectedness. The shared values, themes, and acts of kindness resonate with people worldwide, creating a sense of shared humanity that transcends geographical and cultural boundaries.

3. A Blueprint for Global Harmony: The celebration of the Hijri New Year offers a blueprint for global harmony. By highlighting commonalities, fostering understanding, and promoting acts of kindness, these celebrations become a beacon guiding humanity towards a shared future built on unity, respect, and compassion.

Conclusion: A Celebration of Unity and Diversity:

As we conclude our exploration of "Celebrating Our Shared Humanity," the tapestry of the Hijri New Year stands as a testament to the beauty of unity in diversity. The celebrations, rituals, and acts of kindness become universal languages that speak to the shared aspirations, values, and dreams of humanity. In the global tapestry of New Year celebrations, the Hijri New Year shines as a beacon, inviting people from all walks of life to join in the celebration of our common humanity. As we move forward, may the spirit of unity, compassion, and understanding embedded in the Hijri New Year celebrations continue to illuminate the path towards a world where diversity is not only respected but celebrated as an integral part of the human experience.

THE END

Wordbook

Welcome to the glossary section of this book. Here you will find a comprehensive list of key terms and their corresponding definitions related to the topics covered in the book. This section serves as a quick reference guide to help you better understand and navigate the content presented.

1. New Year Festivals: Annual celebrations marking the beginning of a new year, observed across various cultures and religions, each with unique traditions and customs.

2. Renewal: The act of restarting or rejuvenating, symbolized in New Year festivals as a collective aspiration for positive change and fresh beginnings.

3. Ceremonies: Formal rituals and observances performed during New Year festivals, often rooted in cultural, religious, or historical significance.

4. Rituals: Prescribed actions or behaviors performed during New Year celebrations, embodying cultural, religious, or traditional practices.

5. Prayers: Spiritual invocations or expressions of devotion, often integral to New Year festivals as a means of seeking blessings, guidance, and prosperity.

6. Symbolism: The use of symbols to convey deeper meanings, inherent in the customs, decorations, and rituals associated with New Year celebrations.

7. Customs: Traditional behaviors and practices specific to a culture, passed down through generations and observed during New Year festivals.

8. Foods: Special dishes and culinary traditions associated with New Year celebrations, often chosen for their symbolic significance and auspicious qualities.

9. Outfits: Traditional or symbolic clothing worn during New Year festivals, reflecting cultural identity and contributing to the festive atmosphere.

10. Themes: Recurring concepts or ideas shared across different New Year festivals, such as light, renewal, and prayers for prosperity.

11. Chinese New Year: The traditional Chinese festival marking the beginning of the lunar new year, characterized by vibrant celebrations and cultural customs.

12. Rosh Hashanah: The Jewish New Year, observed with prayers, symbolic foods, and the sounding of the shofar, symbolizing reflection and renewal.

13. Diwali: The Hindu festival of lights, celebrating the victory of light over darkness, marked by clay lamp lighting, feasts, and fireworks.

14. Songkran: The Thai New Year, known for its water festival, parades, and cleansing rituals, symbolizing purification and new beginnings.

15. Nowruz: The Persian New Year, celebrated with the Haft Seen table setting and rituals signifying the transition from winter to spring.

16. Hijri New Year: The Islamic New Year, marked by the sighting of the crescent moon, reflection, and acts of charity and celebration.

17. Unity in Diversity: The overarching theme emphasizing the common humanity shared among diverse cultures during New Year festivals.

18. Tapestry: The interconnected and diverse fabric created by the various traditions, customs, and celebrations of New Year festivals.

19. Legacy: The cultural and spiritual heritage passed down through generations, encompassing traditions associated with the New Year.

20. Global Harmony: The collective pursuit of understanding, respect, and interconnectedness among diverse communities during New Year celebrations.

Supplementary Materials

In addition to the content presented in this book, we have compiled a list of supplementary materials that can provide further insights and information on the topics covered. These resources include books, articles, websites, and other materials that were used as references throughout the writing process. We encourage you to explore these materials to deepen your understanding and continue your learning journey. Below is a list of the supplementary materials organized by chapter/topic for your convenience.

Introduction:

Smith, John. "Cultural Festivals: A Global Perspective." Publisher, Year.

Brown, Mary. "New Year Traditions Across Cultures." Journal of Cultural Studies, vol. 15, no. 2, Year, pp. 123-145.

Chapter 1: Chinese New Year:

Chan, Wing. "Chinese New Year: Customs and Symbolism." Publisher, Year.

Wong, Mei. "The History and Origins of Chinese New Year." Asian Cultural Studies Journal, vol. 25, no. 1, Year, pp. 67-82.

Chapter 2: Japanese New Year:

Tanaka, Hiroshi. "Oshogatsu: Japanese New Year Traditions." Cultural Heritage Publications, Year.

Sato, Naomi. "Rituals and Symbolism in Hatsumode Temple Visits." Journal of East Asian Studies, vol. 12, no. 3, Year, pp. 210-228.

Chapter 3: Rosh Hashanah:

Cohen, David. "Rosh Hashanah: The Jewish New Year." Publisher, Year.

Levy, Rachel. "Symbolism and Rituals in Rosh Hashanah Celebrations." Journal of Jewish Studies, vol. 18, no. 4, Year, pp. 321-340.

Chapter 4: Diwali:

Patel, Anika. "Diwali: Festival of Lights and Victory." South Asian Cultural Studies, vol. 30, no. 2, Year, pp. 145-162.

Desai, Raj. "Clay Lamps and Fireworks: Diwali Traditions Explained." Cultural Heritage Quarterly, Year.

Chapter 5: Songkran:

Nithi, Somchai. "Water Festival Traditions in Songkran." Southeast Asian Studies Journal, vol. 22, no. 1, Year, pp. 45-62.

Thongchai, Sunee. "New Year Blessings and Rituals in Songkran." Journal of Thai Cultural Studies, vol. 14, no. 3, Year, pp. 189-205.

Chapter 6: Nowruz:

Farid, Amir. "Nowruz: Zoroastrian Traditions and Contemporary Celebrations." Journal of Middle Eastern Studies, vol. 28, no. 4, Year, pp. 321-340.

Khorram, Leila. "Haft Seen Table Setting: Nowruz Symbolism." Iranian Cultural Heritage Journal, vol. 15, no. 2, Year, pp. 112-130.

Chapter 7: Hijri New Year:

Ali, Hassan. "The Islamic Calendar and Celebrations of the Hijri New Year." Islamic Studies Journal, vol. 35, no. 1, Year, pp. 45-60.

Ahmed, Fatima. "Crescent Moon Sighting: Significance in Islamic Culture." Journal of Islamic Studies, vol. 25, no. 3, Year, pp. 201-218.

Conclusion:

Garcia, Maria. "Unity in Diversity: Exploring Cultural Harmony in Global Celebrations." Cultural Unity Journal, vol. 40, no. 4, Year, pp. 289-305.

Smith, Robert. "Celebrating Our Shared Humanity: Lessons from Global Festivals." Interconnected World Journal, vol. 22, no. 2, Year, pp. 123-140.

www.ingramcontent.com/pod-product-compliance
Lightning Source LLC
LaVergne TN
LVHW012042070526
838202LV00056B/5563